EAT CHEAPLY AND WELL

EAT CHEAPLY AND WELL

BRENDA SANCTUARY

Illustrated by JON

DAVID & CHARLES

NEWTON ABBOT LONDON NORTH POMFRET (VT) VANCOUVER

ISBN 0 7153 6756 0

Library of Congress Catalog Card Number 74–29017

Set in 11 on 13pt Aldine Bembo and printed in
Great Britain by Latimer Trend & Company Ltd Plymouth
for David & Charles (Holdings) Limited
South Devon House Newton Abbot Devon

Published in the United States of America by
David & Charles Inc
North Pomfret Vermont 05053 USA

Published in Canada by
Douglas David & Charles Limited
132 Philip Avenue North Vancouver BC

Dedicated to
my long-suffering husband, Brian
and my daughters, Charlotte and Siobhan

My very grateful thanks also to Jon for the illustrations, to
Angela Sibley for reading and checking the manuscript and
lastly to Brian for giving me constant encouragement

Abbreviations

tablespoon	tbsp		gram	g
teaspoon	tsp		kilogram	kg
ounce	oz		litre	l
pound	lb		millilitre	ml
pint	pt		centimetre	cm
inch	in			
minute	min			

Measures
Metric measures as used:

1oz 25g
1lb 500g
2pt 1l 125ml

US measures

For the benefit of US readers, where British and American measures differ we have given approximate equivalents. We have tried to use a language common to both countries and, where words differ, have always 'translated' for both sides of the Atlantic!

NB: Imperial measures are always given first—metric, then US follow in brackets.

All recipes are for 4 except where stated.

CONTENTS

INTRODUCTION

I have been most fortunate to have lived in or visited India, the West Indies, Europe, America and the Middle East and have learnt to adapt many dishes to both palate and purse. I have cooked on paraffin cookers in India and canned gas in Italy as well as modern gas and electric cookers in England. Experience has taught me to be brave and experiment with new recipes.

In writing this book my objective has been to provide the opportunity for each reader to make more of the food he or she buys. Many people are unaware that they can eat well yet their meals need not be as expensive as they imagine. The shops are full of convenience foods, tinned, frozen and freeze-dried and, whereas these are useful to have in the house for an emergency and in many cases speed, it is obviously very much cheaper to buy fruit and vegetables when in season; though with heated greenhouses and imports, there no longer seems to be a season for some of them. Fresh fruit and vegetables often take time to prepare but it is well worth the trouble.

I also recommend you to think carefully before throwing away any food. This can be a big money saver because, with imagination, left-over food can be turned into another dish, the most obvious example being shepherd's pie, from the remains of a joint. Many of the recipes in this book started in just this way and, if any left-overs can't be used to create a specific meal, there is always soup; my family nearly left me when they discovered we had 36 litres of my home-made soup in the deep-freeze!

I have devoted one chapter to pasta and rice, which are very underrated in this country, often being considered as secondary foods. Both are full of protein, and, when served as a main dish, can be really economical. Pasta and rice are both useful in that they can be recooked and many of the recipes I have given can be made with pre-cooked pasta and rice.

I often try and decide which piece of kitchen equipment I value most, the one which saves me money and time; there is no doubt that this item is my liquidiser. I use it almost daily for chopping nuts, parsley, mint, etc; making breadcrumbs from toast, fresh bread, biscuits and cake; using these last two as topping for puddings instead of a crumble pastry. The liquidiser is my greatest stand-by for soups and sauces, making mayonnaise so easy to prepare. With a liquidiser, some left-over vegetables and some stock you have a superb thick soup, and with stewed fruit the choice of fruit fool is limitless.

My next favourite, a present from my daughters, is an infra-red grill, which saves a great deal of cooking time and reduces the meat shrinkage. An infra-red grill is ideal for those on a diet as it needs only a brushing of oil and the meat is therefore cooked in its own juices. Also, these little grills are no longer very expensive.

My third choice is the deep-freeze. I have no doubt that in the past four years I have been able to save money purely as a result of this. This is because I do not fill the deep-freeze with ready-prepared branded products but with my own home-made dishes; I stock it with soups, sauces, pasta and rice dishes, casseroles, pâtés, puddings and pastry. If there is any left-over food into the deep-freeze it goes to be used another day, even small amounts of white sauce can be used as a basis for a vol-au-vent filling with mushrooms, chicken, onions or shrimps.

Throughout this book there is an asterisk against the dishes that can be deep-frozen. When freezing food, remember to freeze in the quantities you will need later and in foil containers, so that you only have to put the containers on to a baking sheet and into the oven when the dish has been de-frosted. If the recipe tells you to add cream, etc, or garnish the dish before serving, do this *after* de-frosting and not before freezing. When you want to use the dish, allow time for de-frosting, then re-heat, if the dish is pre-cooked and is to be served hot. In the case of plain pasta, de-frost, then heat in boiling water, drain and toss in hot oil, melted butter or melted margarine. After de-frosting plain rice, toss in hot oil until it is well coated.

I have included many favourites in this recipe book, such as my grandmother's bread pudding, Queen of Puddings and Poor Knights of Windsor; this latter is found in many foreign countries but named quite differently—Pain Perdu in France, Arme Ritter in Germany, Bombay Toast in India and Pan de Santa Teresa or Torrijas in Spain.

When writing the recipes I have not put any measurements for salt or pepper in the ingredients as I believe that these are entirely up to the individual cook and it is a matter of taste. I personally prefer to use ground sea salt. I also use black peppercorns, grinding them, as I find both these give a better flavour to my food.

I have also put only an approximate preparation time, as this too is up to each individual. Preparation depends so much on your kitchen and how organised you are; some people might prepare the dish in half the time, others may take longer. If you have labour-saving equipment such as a mixer or liquidiser then, of course, the time is lessened and while the mixer or liquidiser is busy working, you can be doing another job.

Cooking is easy and fun if you follow this advice—never panic. Choose your recipe, read it carefully, then get all the necessary ingredients and utensils ready, allowing yourself plenty of time to prepare and cook the dish. I do hope you enjoy trying out the recipes in this book.

PASTRY AND BATTER

Shortcrust*

8oz (250g, 2 cups) plain flour
4oz (100g, ½ cup) fat

Preparation time: about 30min
Sift the flour and a pinch of salt into a large bowl. Cut the fat into the flour. Rub the flour and fat together with the finger tips until the mixture resembles fine breadcrumbs. Add enough cold water to make into a stiff dough. Roll out the pastry on a floured board. Use the pastry as required. Makes enough to line an 8in pie dish.

Flaky Pastry*

8oz (250g, 2 cups) plain flour
6oz (150g, ¾ cup) butter
½ tbsp (7ml, ¾ tbsp) lemon juice

Preparation time: about 1hr
Sift the flour and a large pinch of salt into a large bowl. Using the finger tips, rub a quarter of the butter into the flour until the mixture resembles fine breadcrumbs. Add the lemon juice and enough cold water to make into a soft dough. Turn the dough out on to a floured board and roll the pastry out into an oblong shape about ½in (1¼cm) thick. Soften a third of the remaining butter and dab it on to two-thirds of the pastry. Keeping the pastry edge square, fold the pastry into three by folding over one-third towards the centre and the bottom third over the top. Give the pastry half a turn and roll out again, then fold again as before. Wrap the pastry in greaseproof paper and leave in a

cold place for 20min. Using the remaining butter, repeat the process for four rolls and turns, allowing 20min rest in a cold place after two rolls. Finally roll the pastry out and use as required. Makes enough to line an 8in pie dish.

Batter

4 oz (100g, 1 cup) flour
½ pt (250ml, 1¼ cups) milk
1 egg

Preparation time: about 40min
Sift the flour and a pinch of salt into a large bowl, and make a well in the centre of the flour. Break the egg into the well and add a little of the milk, mixing from the centre. Make a smooth batter, slowly adding half the milk as you mix. When all the flour is blended, add the rest of the milk. Beat well to allow the air to circulate. Leave to stand for 30min.

SAUCES AND DRESSINGS

Savoury White Sauce*

1 pt (500ml, 2½ cups) milk
2oz (50g, 4 tbsp) butter
2oz (50g, ½ cup) flour
2oz (50g) onions
4 peppercorns

Preparation time: about 15min   Cooking time: 25min

Peel the onion and put into a saucepan with the milk and peppercorns. Leave to simmer for 10min. Strain the milk. Make a roux by melting the butter in a thick bottomed saucepan, remove from the heat and stir in the flour. When blended, pour in the milk, stirring all the time. Return the saucepan to the stove and stirring all the time allow the sauce to thicken. Stirring, simmer the sauce for a further 10min.

Mayonnaise

2 egg yolks
½pt (250ml, 1¼ cups) olive oil
½ tsp (3g, ¾ tsp) salt
½ tsp (3g, ¾ tsp) dry mustard
1 tbsp (15ml, 1¼ tbsp) lemon juice or wine vinegar

Preparation time: about 30min

Beat the egg yolks in a bowl until thick. Add the salt, dry mustard and lemon juice or vinegar. Beat for a further minute. Continue beating, add the olive oil, drop by drop, until half the olive oil has been used, then, still beating, pour the oil into the mixture in a steady stream until the mayonnaise is thick.

Parsley Sauce, Cheese Sauce, Shrimp Sauce*

Make 1pt (500ml, 2½ cups) basic white sauce as above, then stir in main ingredients—2 tbsp (20g, 2½ tbsp) chopped parsley, or 2oz (50g) grated Cheddar cheese, or ½pt (175g, 6oz) peeled shrimps—and continue simmering for a further 10min.

Egg and Lemon Sauce

4 egg yolks
3 tbsp (50ml, 4 tbsp) hot stock
4 tbsp (65ml, ⅓ cup) lemon juice

Preparation time: about 10min   Cooking time: 15min

Whisk the egg yolks until light and fluffy, then gradually whisk in the lemon juice. When the eggs and lemon juice are blended, add the hot stock, whisking all the time. Put the mixture into a thick bottomed saucepan and gently heat but do not boil. Stir all the time until the sauce thickens. Serve hot.

Sweet and Sour Sauce

1 tbsp (15ml, 1¼ tbsp) soya sauce
1oz (25g, scant ⅓ cup) cornflour
2 tbsp (25ml, 2½ tbsp) vinegar
1oz (25g, ¼ cup) brown sugar
1 red pepper
½pt (250ml, 1¼ cup) pineapple juice
4oz (100g) young carrots
3 tbsp (50ml, 4 tbsp) olive oil

Preparation time: about 30min   Cooking time: 10min

Peel and finely grate the carrots. Remove the core and seeds from the red pepper, then finely slice it. Blend together the soya sauce, cornflour, vinegar, brown sugar, pineapple juice and 2 tbsp (3 tbsp) of olive oil. Simmer gently for 5min.

Heat the remaining oil and fry the carrots and red pepper for 5min. Add to the sauce and stir well.

Tomato Sauce*

8oz (250g) soft tomatoes
3 tbsp (60ml, 3¾ tbsp) tomato purée
1 tbsp (15ml, 1¼ tbsp) Worcestershire sauce
1 tsp (5g, 1¼ tsp) dry mustard
2 tbsp (25ml, 2½ tbsp) wine vinegar
½oz (15g, 1 tbsp) butter
1 tsp (5g, 1¼ tsp) salt
1 tsp (5g, 1¼ tsp) paprika pepper

Preparation time: about 20min   Cooking time: 20min

Skin the tomatoes and cut into quarters. Put all the ingredients into a thick bottomed saucepan and simmer, stirring for 20min. Rub the mixture through a sieve and serve hot.

Sauce Bolognese*

8oz (250g, 1 cup) minced beef
4oz (100g) onions
1 garlic clove
2 tbsp (40ml, 2½ tbsp) tomato purée
8oz (250g) soft tomatoes
¼pt (125ml, scant ¾ cup) stock
½ gill (60ml, ⅓ cup) olive oil
1 tsp (5g, 1¼ tsp) sugar

Preparation time: about 20min   Cooking time: 35min

Skin and finely chop the tomatoes. Peel and finely chop the onions and garlic. Heat the oil and cook the onions until soft, then add the meat and brown. Add the rest of the ingredients and salt and pepper to taste. Simmer gently for 30min. Serve with pasta (see page 96).

Tartare Sauce

½pt (250ml, 1¼ cups) mayonnaise
1 tbsp (10g, 1¼ tbsp) capers
1 tbsp (10g, 1¼ tbsp) chopped gherkins
1 tbsp (10g, 1¼ tbsp) chopped chives

Preparation time: about 30min
Add the capers, gherkins and chives to the mayonnaise. Serve with fish and fried chicken.

French Dressing

4 tbsp (65ml, ⅓ cup) olive oil
2 tbsp (25ml, 2½ tbsp) wine vinegar
1 tsp (3g, 1¼ tsp) sugar
1 tsp (3g, 1¼ tsp) salt

Preparation time: 15min
Mix together the sugar and salt, and add a pinch of pepper and dry mustard. Stir in the vinegar and olive oil. Mix well.

STARTERS

Cucumber and Sour Cream Salad

1 cucumber
½pt (250ml, 1¼ cups) sour cream
1 garlic clove
1 lemon

Preparation time: about 50min
Peel the cucumber and cut into small dice. Sprinkle with salt and leave
for 30min. Squeeze the juice from the lemon. Drain the liquid from
the cucumber. Crush the clove of garlic, mix into the sour cream and
add the lemon juice. Add pepper to taste. Stir the cucumber into the
sour cream and chill.

Orange and Paprika Pepper Salad

2 oranges
1 head chicory
6oz (150g, ¾ cup) cottage cheese
1 tbsp (15ml, 1½ tbsp) lemon juice
1 green pepper
2oz (50g) onions

Preparation time: about 25min   Time to chill: 30min
Peel and remove any pith from the oranges, then carefully divide them
into segments. Finely chop the onion. Remove the centre core and
seeds from the green pepper, slice into rings. Slice the chicory and
sprinkle with the lemon juice. Mix together the cottage cheese, onion
and chicory. Add salt to taste. Put the cottage cheese mixture on to a
plate. Arrange the orange segments and green pepper rings round the
cheese. Sprinkle with paprika pepper. Chill for 30min.

Tomatoes with Egg and Lemon Sauce

8oz (250g) tomatoes
1oz (25g, 2 tbsp) butter
4 egg yolks
3 tbsp (50ml, 4 tbsp) hot stock
4 tbsp (65ml, ⅓ cup) lemon juice

Preparation time: about 30min   Cooking time: 30min

Skin and slice the tomatoes and arrange in a shallow dish. Sprinkle with salt and pepper and dot with the butter. Put the dish in a moderate oven, 350° F, 180° C, mark 4 for 30min. While the tomatoes are cooking make the sauce (see page 14). Pour the sauce over the tomatoes and serve hot.

Guacamole

2 avocado pears
2oz (50g) onions
5oz (125g, scant ¾ cup) cream cheese
2 lemons

Preparation time: about 30min

Peel and finely grate the onion. Squeeze the juice from the lemons. Cut the avocado pears in half and remove the stones. Scoop out the pulp and mash until soft. Mix together the avocado pulp, grated onion, cream cheese and lemon juice. Add salt and black pepper to taste. Chill. Serve as a dip.

Taramasalata*

8oz (250g) smoked cod's roe
1 clove garlic, crushed
8oz (250g) white bread
1 lemon
olive oil

Preparation time: about 30min

Cut the crusts from the bread, put it into a bowl and cover with water. When the bread is thoroughly soaked, squeeze dry. Pound the cod's roe in a mortar and add the crushed garlic. Stir in the bread, add a little olive oil and mix well. Continue adding lemon juice and olive oil while stirring until the mixture is a smooth, creamy purée. Put the mixture into a bowl and chill. Serve with hot toast.

Bismarck Herrings

4 herrings
1 tbsp (10g, 1¼ tbsp) salt
3 bay leaves
1pt (500ml, 2½ cups) white wine vinegar
1pt (500ml, 2½ cups) water
1 chilli pepper
1 tbsp (10g, 1¼ tbsp) pickling spice
4oz (100g) onions

Preparation time: about 1hr and a day   Cooking time: 5min
Bone and clean the herrings, then put them into a shallow dish. Mix
together the water and salt and pour over the herrings. Leave for 1hr.
Peel and slice the onion. Put the spice and wine vinegar into a saucepan,
bring to the boil and remove from the stove. Leave for 30min. Strain
and allow to get cold. Remove the herrings from the brine and put
them into a shallow dish with the bayleaves, onions and chilli pepper.
Pour on the vinegar and leave for a day. Remove the herrings from the
liquid and serve cold.

Jellied Eggs

4 eggs
¼pt (125ml, ½ cup) chicken stock
2 tbsp (25ml, 2½ tbsp) sherry
1 green pepper
2 tsp (10g, 3 tsp) gelatine
2 tbsp (25ml, 2½ tbsp) lemon juice
1 tomato
4 tbsp (65ml, ⅓ cup) hot water

Preparation time: about 25min   Cooking time: 10min

Dissolve the gelatine in the hot water. When thoroughly dissolved mix into the chicken stock. Add the sherry and lemon juice. Strain through a fine nylon sieve. Leave to thicken. Boil the eggs for 10min. Plunge into cold water and when cold remove the shells. Cut off the top of the pepper, remove the centre core and seeds. Cut the pepper and tomato into thin rings. Oil 4 ramekin dishes and pour a little gelatine into each dish. Leave to set. Put a tomato ring into each dish, then a pepper ring, cover with a little more gelatine and leave to set. Put an egg in each dish and cover with the remaining gelatine. Leave to set for 3hr. When set, turn the jellied eggs out and serve with a salad.

Stuffed Eggs with Onions

4 eggs
½ tsp (2g, 1 tsp) curry powder
¼ tbsp (5g, 1 tbsp) chopped parsley
2oz (50g) onions
1 tbsp (20ml, 1½ tbsp) mayonnaise
8 anchovy fillets

Preparation time: about 15min   Cooking time: 10min

Boil the eggs for 10min. Plunge into cold water and remove shells. Cut the eggs into two. Remove the yolks and mash them with a fork. Peel and finely chop the onion. Mix together the egg yolks, onion, curry powder, mayonnaise and chopped parsley. Add salt and pepper to taste. Fill the centres of the eggs with the onion mixture. Garnish with an anchovy fillet.

Prawn Cocktail

1pt (350g, ¾lb) cooked prawns
1 tbsp (20ml, 1¼ tbsp) tomato purée
1 small lettuce
½pt (250ml, 1¼ cups) yogurt

Preparation time: about 20min

Clean the lettuce and rinse in cold water. Chop finely. Clean the prawns, removing the shells and the black vein. Mix together the yogurt and tomato purée, adding salt and paprika pepper to taste. Add the prawns and mix well. Divide the lettuce into four small dishes and put equal amounts of prawns into each dish. Serve chilled.

Prawn Surprise

1pt (350g, ¾lb) prawns
4oz (100g) tomatoes
3 eggs
4oz (100g) onions
1pt (500ml, 2½ cups) milk
2oz (50g, 4 tbsp) butter
2oz (50g, ½ cup) cornflour or flour
4 peppercorns

Preparation time: about 30min   Cooking time: 1hr 15min

Boil the eggs for 10min. Plunge into cold water and remove the shells. Peel and finely slice half the onions. Skin and finely slice the tomatoes. Slice the eggs. Remove the shells and black vein from the prawns. Grease a 6in soufflé dish. Put the eggs, tomatoes and onions in layers in the dish, sprinkling each layer with salt and pepper. Add the prawns to the soufflé dish. Make a white sauce with the milk, butter, cornflour or flour, peppercorns and remaining onion (see page 13). Pour the sauce over the prawns. Cover the dish with foil and place in a roasting pan. Pour hot water into the pan so that it comes half way up the side of the soufflé dish. Cook in a slow oven, 300° F, 150° C, mark 2 for 45min. Serve hot.

Eggs Baked with Turkey

4 eggs
6oz (150g) cooked turkey
2oz (50g) cheese
1oz (25g, 2 tbsp) butter

Preparation time: about 10min   Cooking time: 4–5min
Grate the cheese. Cut the turkey into small pieces. Grease 4 individual
ramekin dishes with the butter, and divide the turkey amongst them.
Break one egg into each dish, adding a pinch of salt and pepper. Cover
with the cheese, sprinkle with paprika pepper. Bake in a hot oven,
400° F, 205° C, mark 6, for 4–5min. Serve hot.

Liver Pâté*

6oz (150g) chicken liver
3oz (75g) pork liver
5oz (125g, scant ¾ cup) unsalted butter
1 garlic clove
2oz (50g) onions

Preparation time: about 30min and overnight   Cooking time:
                                                         15–20min
Cut the livers in half and remove any coarse tubes. Peel and finely chop
the onion. Peel and crush the garlic. Mix together. Melt 1 tbsp (1½ tbsp)
butter and fry the onion and garlic until transparent. Add the livers and
fry them until they are firm. Remove the livers from the pan and leave
to cool. Melt 3 tbsp (4 tbsp) of butter. Rub the liver and onions
through a fine sieve, add the melted butter and salt and pepper to taste.
Mix well. Put into a greased mould. Melt the remaining butter and
pour on top of the pâté. Leave overnight in the refrigerator. Serve with
hot toast.

SOUPS

Basic Meat Stock*

4oz (100g) onions
2 garlic cloves
2 tsp (8g, 2½ tsp) salt
6 peppercorns
2 bouquet garni bunches
4oz (100g) carrots
bones

Preparation time: about 15min   Cooking time: 3hr
Put the bones (any meat or chicken) into a large saucepan. Peel the
onions, garlic and carrots, slice and put into the saucepan with the
bones. Add the salt, peppercorns and bouquet garni sprigs (see below).
Fill the saucepan with cold water and bring to the boil, then allow to
simmer for 3hr. Strain the stock through a fine sieve and cool.

Stock will keep for many days in a refrigerator if re-boiled after a
few days.

Bouquet Garni

Tie a bayleaf, sprig of thyme and parsley together in a small piece of
muslin, and use to flavour stock, casseroles, etc.

Basic Fish Stock

4oz (100g) onions
1 garlic clove
2 tsp (8g, 2½ tsp) salt
6 peppercorns
2 bouquet garni bunches
4oz (100g) carrots
1lb (500g) fish, bones, etc

Preparation time: about 20min   Cooking time: 3hr
Put the bones, fish, etc, into a large saucepan. Peel and slice the onions,
carrots and garlic. Put the vegetables, salt, peppercorns, bouquet garni
sprigs and garlic into the saucepan with the fish. Cover with cold water
and bring to the boil, then simmer for 3hr. Strain the stock through a
fine sieve and leave to go cold.

Borsch—Beetroot Soup

12oz (350g) cooked beetroot
8oz (250g) potatoes
4oz (100g) onions
4oz (100g) carrots
12oz (350g) cabbage
1¾pt (1l, 4 cups) stock
1 tbsp (15ml, 1¼ tbsp) vinegar
1oz (25g, 2 tbsp) butter
1 tsp (5g) sugar
1 tbsp (20ml, 1¼ tbsp) tomato purée
¼pt (125ml, scant ¾ cup) sour cream
1 tbsp (10g, 1¼ tbsp) parsley

Preparation time: about 50min   Cooking time: 40min
Peel and finely chop the beetroot, potatoes, onion and carrots. Finely
shred the cabbage. Put the stock into a large saucepan with the beetroot
and vinegar and bring to the boil. Remove from the heat and leave for
20min. Melt the butter and cook the remaining vegetables until soft.
Stir in the tomato purée and sugar with salt and pepper to taste. Add
all these vegetables to the beetroot and stock, bring to the boil and
simmer for a further 30min. Add the parsley and stir well. Serve hot
with a spoonful of sour cream in each bowl.

Cream of Corn Soup*

11½oz (326g) cream-style corn
4oz (100g) onions
¾pt (375ml, 2 cups) milk
¾pt (375ml, 2 cups) vegetable stock
2oz (50g, ½ cup) flour
3oz (75g, 6 tbsp) butter
½ tsp (3g) ground paprika pepper

Preparation time: about 20min   Cooking time: 30min
Peel and finely chop the onion. Melt 1oz (25g, 2 tbsp) of the butter in
a saucepan and cook onion until soft. Add the corn, milk, stock and
paprika pepper. Add salt and pepper to taste and cook over a low heat
for 20min. In another saucepan, melt the rest of the butter, remove

from the heat and stir in the flour until smooth. Stir in 1 tbsp of the soup and, when the sauce is smooth, add the sauce to the soup. Simmer for a further 5min. Serve hot.

French Onion Soup

1lb (500g) onions
2oz (50g, 4 tbsp) butter
1¾pt (1l, 2 cups) stock
1oz (25g, ¼ cup) flour
4 slices French bread
4oz (100g) cheese

Preparation time: about 30min   Cooking time: 15min
Peel and roughly chop the onion. Grate the cheese. Melt the butter in a thick-bottomed saucepan and cook the onion until soft and just brown. Add salt and pepper to taste. Stir in the flour and cook over a low heat for a few minutes. Pour in the stock and bring to the boil, then simmer for 10min. Toast the bread. Put a slice of toast on top of each serving of soup and generously sprinkle with grated cheese. Serve hot.

Lentil Soup*

8oz (250g, 1 cup) split lentils
1 chilli
4oz (100g) onions
1 garlic clove
3½pt (2l, 4pt) water
1oz (25g, 2 tbsp) butter

Preparation time: about 2hr   Cooking time: 40–45min
Put the lentils into a large bowl, cover with cold water and leave
for 2hr. Strain. Finely slice the chilli. Peel and finely chop the onion
and garlic. Put half the onion and chilli into a large saucepan, add the
lentils and water, bring to the boil and simmer for 40min. Rub the
lentils and liquid through a sieve into a large saucepan. Melt the butter
and cook the remaining onion, chilli and garlic until soft. Rub through
a sieve and stir into the lentil mixture. Add salt and pepper to taste.
Reheat and serve hot.

Minestrone

2oz (50g, ⅓ cup) haricot beans
4oz (100g) carrots
4oz (100g) potatoes
4oz (100g) tomatoes
1 celery stick
2oz (50g) onions
8oz (250g) cabbage
3oz (75g) bacon
1 garlic clove
2oz (50g) peas
1qt (1l 125ml, 2½pt) meat stock
2oz (50g, 4 tbsp) dripping
2oz (50g, ¼ cup) Parmesan cheese
2oz (50g, ⅓ cup) long grain rice

Preparation time: overnight and about 30min
                              Cooking time: 2hr and 45min
Soak the haricot beans overnight in cold salted water. Next day, strain
and put the beans into fresh water and cook until tender, about 2hr.

Strain the beans and put aside. Peel and finely dice the carrots, potato and onion. Skin and chop the tomatoes. Peel and chop the garlic. Finely shred the cabbage and slice the celery. Remove the rind and chop the bacon. Grate the Parmesan cheese. Melt the dripping in a large saucepan, add the bacon, onion and garlic and cook until the onions are soft. Add the meat stock, salt and pepper to taste. Bring to the boil. Add the carrots, potato, cabbage and celery and simmer for 10min. Add the rice, peas, tomatoes and haricot beans and simmer for a further 30min. Serve hot with Parmesan cheese sprinkled over each serving.

Potage Parmentière

1lb (500g) potatoes
2 leeks
2oz (50g, 4 tbsp) butter
1pt (500ml, 2½ cups) water
¼pt (125ml, scant ¾ cup) cream
½pt (250ml, 1¼ cups) milk
1 egg yolk

Preparation time: about 30min   Cooking time: 35min

Peel and slice the potatoes. Slice the leeks. Melt the butter in a saucepan and cook the leeks until soft. Add the potatoes, stock and salt and pepper to taste. Cook for 20min until the potatoes are soft. Rub the potatoes, leeks and liquid through a sieve. Add the milk to the potato soup, bring to the boil and simmer gently for 5min. Whisk the egg yolk until light and fluffy then stir into the cream. Stir the mixture into the soup and simmer for a further 5min. Serve with:

Croûtons

4oz (100g) bread
¼pt (125ml, scant ¾ cup) oil

Preparation time: about 10min   Cooking time: 5min

Cut the bread into very small cubes. Heat the oil and fry the cubes of bread until brown. Drain on kitchen paper. Serve hot or cold.

Tomato Soup*

1lb (500g) tomatoes
4oz (100g) onions
1 tbsp (10g, 1¼ tbsp) flour
2 tsp (5g, 2½ tsp) sugar
1 tbsp (10g, 1¼ tbsp) chopped parsley
1oz (25g, 2 tbsp) butter
1¾pt (1l, 4 cups) stock
¼pt (125ml, scant ¾ cup) single cream

Preparation time: about 20min   Cooking time: 40min

Peel and finely chop the onion. Skin and finely chop the tomatoes. Melt the butter in a large saucepan and cook the onion until soft. Sprinkle in the flour and continue cooking for 3min. Add the tomatoes, sugar, parsley and salt and pepper to taste. Simmer for 20min. Add the stock and, stirring all the time, continue cooking for a further 15min. Rub the soup through a sieve into a large saucepan. Reheat and stir in the cream. Serve hot with croûtons (see page 30).

Watercress Soup*

4 bunches watercress
4oz (100g) onions
8oz (250g) potatoes
2 garlic cloves
3pt (1l 625ml, 7½ cups) chicken stock
¼pt (125ml, scant ¾ cup) single cream

Preparation time: about 20min   Cooking time: 25min
Chilling time: 2hr

Peel and finely chop the onions and potatoes. Remove the stalks from the watercress and put all the ingredients except the cream into a large saucepan. Bring to the boil, then simmer gently for 25min. Rub through a sieve into a large bowl, add salt and pepper to taste. Chill in a refrigerator. Stir in the cream just before serving.
Can also be served hot.

Scotch Broth

1lb (500g) stewing beef or neck of mutton
4oz (100g) onions
4oz (100g) carrots
8oz (250g) turnips
1 leek
1½oz (37g, ¼ cup) pearl barley
2oz (50g, ⅓ cup) dried peas
2½pt (1l 375ml, 6¼ cups) water
1 tbsp (10g, 1¼ tbsp) chopped parsley

Preparation time: about 30min   Cooking time: 3hr

Peel and dice the carrot and turnip. Peel and finely chop the onion.
Cut the leek into thick slices. Wash the pearl barley in cold water.
Wipe the meat and put in a large saucepan with the pearl barley, salt
and pepper to taste and the water. Bring to the boil and skim. Simmer
for 1hr. Add the onion, carrot, turnip, leek and dried peas. Simmer
for a further 1½hr, or until the meat is tender. Remove the meat and
skim the broth. Add the chopped parsley. Serve hot.

The meat can either be served separately as a main course or in the
broth cut into small pieces.

Vichyssoise—Cold Potato and Leek Soup

1lb (500g) potatoes
4oz (100g) onions
3 leeks
2oz (50g, 4 tbsp) butter
1¾pt (1l, 4 cups) chicken stock
1 garlic clove
¼pt (125ml, scant ¾ cup) single cream
1 tbsp (10g, 1¼ tbsp) chopped chives

Preparation time: about 20min   Cooking time: 30min
Chilling time: 2hr

Peel and finely chop the onions and garlic. Roughly chop the leeks. Peel and slice the potatoes. Melt the butter in a saucepan and cook the onions and leeks until soft. Add the potatoes and stock and cook until soft—about 25min. Rub through a sieve and add salt and pepper to taste. Leave to go cold. Stir in the cream. Garnish with chopped chives.
Can also be served hot.

Chilled Carrot Soup*

1½lb (750g) carrots
4 celery sticks
6oz (150g) onions
1 garlic clove
2 tbsp (20g, 2½ tbsp) chopped parsley
2pt (1l 125ml, 5 cups) chicken stock
2 bay leaves
¼pt (125ml, scant ¾ cup) single cream

Preparation time: about 30min   Cooking time: 20min
Chilling time: 2hr

Peel and slice the carrots and onions. Slice the celery. Peel and crush the garlic. Put the carrots, celery, onions, garlic, bay leaves and stock into a large saucepan. Cook for 20min. Rub through a fine sieve into a large bowl, add salt and pepper to taste. Stir in the chopped parsley. Leave to chill in the refrigerator. Just before serving, stir in the cream.
Can also be served hot.

C   33

Cold Cucumber Soup*

2 cucumbers
4oz (100g) onions
1 tbsp (10g, 1¼ tbsp) chopped parsley
1oz (25g, 2 tbsp) butter
1oz (25g, ¼ cup) flour
1pt (500ml, 2½ cups) milk
1pt (500ml, 2½ cups) stock
¼pt (125ml, scant ¾ cup) single cream

Preparation time: about 20min   Cooking time: 30min
Chilling time: 2hr

Peel the cucumbers and onions, chop finely. Make a smooth paste with the flour and 2 tbsp (25ml, 2½ tbsp) milk. Put the remaining milk and stock into a saucepan, add the cucumber and onion and simmer over a low heat until the cucumber is tender. Rub the cucumber, onion and liquid through a sieve into a large saucepan, add the chopped parsley, butter and salt and pepper to taste. Stir in the flour and simmer for 10min. Chill. Just before serving, stir in the cream.

Gazpacho (Andalusian Iced Soup)

8oz (250g) tomatoes
1 cucumber
2oz (50g) green pepper
2 garlic cloves
4oz (100g, 1½ cups) dry breadcrumbs
3 tbsp (50ml, 4 tbsp) olive oil
1pt (500ml, 2½ cups) water
1 tbsp (15ml, 1¼ tbsp) vinegar
8oz (250g) ice cubes

Preparation time: about 30min   Chilling time: 1hr

Skin and dice the tomatoes. Peel and dice the cucumber and onion. Remove the stalk, core and seeds from the green pepper and dice finely. Peel and pound the garlic in a large bowl, add the breadcrumbs and vinegar and salt and pepper to taste. Mix well and add the olive oil drop by drop until a smooth paste is formed. Put the paste into a soup tureen, add the diced vegetables and stir. Pour in the water and add the ice cubes. Leave until the ice has melted. Serve very cold.

Jellied Consommé

2pt (1l 125ml, 5 cups) beef stock
1lb (500g) tomatoes
2oz (50g) onions
1 celery stick
4oz (100g) turnips
4 peppercorns
6oz (150g) minced beef
2 egg whites
2 egg shells
1 bunch bouquet garni

Preparation time: about 30min   Cooking time: 50min
Setting time: 4hr

Cut the tomatoes in half. Peel and chop the onion and the turnip.
Cut the celery into 4. Put the beef stock, tomatoes, onion, celery,
turnip and peppercorns into a saucepan, add salt to taste and a bouquet
garni, and simmer for 20min. Lightly whisk the egg whites and crush
the shells. Add the meat, egg whites and shells to the soup, whisk and
bring to the boil. Leave to simmer for 30min. Strain through a fine
muslin cloth into a large bowl. Put the soup into the refrigerator and
leave to set. Cut into cubes and serve garnished with chopped chives.

FISH

Plaice with Almonds

2lb (1kg) plaice fillets
1pt (500ml, 2½ cups) milk
2oz (50g) onions
1 garlic clove
1 bay leaf
4 peppercorns
4oz (100g, ½ cup) butter
2oz (50g, ½ cup) flour
2oz (50g, scant ⅓ cup) split almonds
¼pt (125ml, scant ¾ cup) single cream

Preparation time: about 45min   Cooking time: 35min

Peel the onion and put it into a saucepan with the milk, garlic, bay leaf and peppercorns. Bring to the boil, then remove the pan from the stove and leave for 30min. Put the plaice fillets into a shallow casserole, dot with 2oz (50g) butter and sprinkle with salt and pepper. Cover with lid or foil and put into a moderately hot oven, 400° F, 205° C, mark 6, for 15min. Strain the milk and make a white sauce (see page 13) with the remaining butter and flour. Add the cream and almonds to the sauce and stirring cook for a further 5min. Pour the sauce over the plaice and serve hot.

Plaice Rice Bake

2lb (1kg) plaice fillets
4oz (100g, ½ cup) long grain rice
2oz (50g) onions
1 tbsp (10g, 1¼ tbsp) dried red and green peppers
¾pt (375ml, 2 cups) water
½pt (250ml, 1¼ cups) milk
2oz (50g, 4 tbsp) butter
2oz (50g) Cheddar cheese
1 tsp (5g, 1¼ tsp) salt

Preparation time: about 30min   Cooking time: 30min

Grate the cheese. Bring the water to the boil in a large saucepan, add the salt and sprinkle in the rice and pepper flakes. Bring to the boil again and simmer for 20min, or until the rice has absorbed all the liquid.

While the rice is cooking, put the plaice fillets in a shallow casserole and pour over the milk, dot with half the butter and add salt and pepper to taste. Cook in a moderately hot oven, 350° F, 180° C, mark 4, for 10min. Drain the fish and put aside to keep hot. Put the rice into a shallow casserole, lay the plaice fillets on top of the rice, dot with the remaining butter, cover with the grated cheese and put into a moderate oven, 300° F, 150° C, mark 3, to cook for 10min.

Cod Steaks with Shrimp Sauce

2lb (1kg) cod steaks
4oz (100g) butter
Sauce
¾pt (375ml, 2 cups) milk
2oz (50g, ½ cup) flour
2oz (50g, 4 tbsp) butter
¼pt (125ml, scant ¾ cup) single cream
¼pt (175g, 6oz) shrimps

Preparation time: about 30min   Cooking time: 30min

Melt the butter and brush over the cod steaks. Sprinkle with salt and pepper. Put the steaks in the grill pan and cook under a hot grill for 10min, then place on a hot serving plate and keep hot. Make a shrimp sauce (see page 14). Stir the cream into the sauce and pour over the cod.

Puffy Cod Fillets

2oz (50g, scant ⅓ cup) blanched almonds
2lb (1kg) cod fillets
3oz (75g, 6 tbsp) butter
½pt (250ml, 1¼ cups) milk
½pt (250ml, 1¼ cups) natural yogurt
3 egg whites

Preparation time: about 30min   Cooking time: 30min

Finely chop the almonds. Grease a shallow casserole. Put the cod fillets on the bottom of the casserole, dot with butter and pour over the milk.

Add salt and pepper to taste, cover the casserole with foil and cook in a moderate oven, 350° F, 180° C, mark 4, for 25min. Whisk the egg whites until stiff, fold in the yogurt and pour over the fish. Sprinkle on the chopped almonds. Put the casserole back into the oven and cook for a further 5min.

Baked Cod in Cider

2lb (1kg) cod
¾pt (375ml, 2 cups) cider
2 tbsp (50g, 2½ tbsp) chopped parsley
8oz (250g) tomatoes

Preparation time: about 20min　　　　　　Cooking time: 30min
Clean the fish and sprinkle with salt and pepper. Skin and slice the tomatoes. Lay the fish in a shallow casserole and arrange the tomatoes on top with the parsley. Pour over the cider and cook in a moderately hot oven, 400° F, 205° C, mark 6, for 30min.

Smoked Cod Pie*

2lb (1kg) smoked cod
2 eggs
1½lb (750g) potatoes
2oz (50g, ¾ cup) dried breadcrumbs
2oz (50g, 4 tbsp) butter
1 tsp (5g, 1¼ tsp) dried thyme

Preparation time: about 30min　　　　　　　Cooking time: 40min

Whisk the eggs thoroughly. Peel the potatoes and cook in boiling water for 20min. Meanwhile put the smoked cod in a roasting tin and cover with water. Cook in a moderately hot oven, 400° F, 205° C, mark 6, for 15min. Drain and flake the cod. Drain and mash the potatoes, add the butter and beat well. Add the flaked fish, eggs and thyme, and salt and pepper to taste. Stir well. Put the mixture into a greased pie dish, cover with the breadcrumbs and cook in a moderate oven, 350° F, 180° C, mark 4, for 20min.

Fish Fillets Baked with Bananas

4 cod or haddock fillets
3 tbsp (50ml, 3¾ tbsp) tomato purée
4 bananas
2oz (50g, ¼ cup) sugar
3 tbsp (50ml, 4 tbsp) olive oil
½ pt (250ml, 1¼ cups) water
1 tsp (5g, 1¼ tsp) dried basil
1 tbsp (10g, 1¼ tbsp) chopped parsley

Preparation time: about 20min　　　　　　　Cooking time: 35min

Grease a shallow casserole and put in the fish. Sprinkle the fillets with salt, pepper, dried basil and parsley. Blend together the tomato purée, sugar, water and olive oil. Peel the bananas and slice in half lengthways. Put the bananas on top of the fish and pour over the sauce. Cover the casserole with greaseproof paper and cook in a moderate oven, 350° F, 180° C, mark 4, for 35min. Serve hot.

Fillets of Haddock in Orange Baskets

2lb (1kg) haddock fillets
2 tbsp (25ml, 2½ tbsp) lemon juice
½pt (250ml, 1¼ cups) milk and water
4 large oranges
½pt (250ml, 1¼ cups) milk
1oz (25g, ¼ cup) flour
1oz (25g, 2 tbsp) butter

Preparation time: about 40min   Cooking time: 35min

Trim the fillets and sprinkle with salt, pepper and lemon juice. Roll them up and put into a shallow casserole. Pour on the ½pt (250ml, 1¼ cups) milk and water and cook in a moderate oven, 350° F, 180° C, mark 4, for 25min. Cut the oranges in half and scoop out the pulp. Remove the pith and cut the pulp into small pieces. Make a white sauce (see page 13) with the milk, flour and butter. Remove the saucepan from the stove and stir in the orange pulp and juice. Put half a fillet of haddock into each orange shell and pour some sauce over the top of the fish. Cook under a hot grill for 2–3min to brown the top lightly. Serve hot.

New England Fish Chowder

2lb (1kg) haddock
1lb (500g) potatoes
4oz (100g) onions
4oz (100g) salt pork or bacon
1pt (500ml, 2½ cups) milk

Preparation time: about 30min   Cooking time: 45min

Peel and slice the potatoes and onions. Put the fish into a large saucepan, add salt and cover with water. Cook for 20min, then remove the fish from the saucepan and keep warm. Put the potatoes into the fish stock and cook for 15min. While the potatoes are cooking, roughly chop the salt pork or bacon then fry until the fat runs out. Add the onion and fry until golden brown. Put the fish, meat and onion into the saucepan with the potatoes and stock, adding milk and salt and pepper to taste. Re-heat and serve in a large soup tureen with cream crackers.

Bishop's Stew

2lb (1kg) cod or haddock
4oz (100g) onions
8oz (250g) potatoes
4oz (100g) tomatoes
2 green peppers
2pt (1l 125ml, 5 cups) fish stock or water
1 tbsp (10g, 1¼ tbsp) paprika pepper
¼pt (125ml, scant ¾ cup) olive oil
2 bay leaves
3 garlic cloves

Preparation time: about 30min   Cooking time: 45min

Peel and slice the onions and potatoes. Skin and slice the tomatoes. Remove the centre core and seeds from the green pepper, then slice. Cut the fish into medium sized cubes. Put the olive oil into a deep frying pan, add the onions and cook until soft. Add all the vegetables, bay leaves, peeled and crushed garlic, and salt and pepper to taste. Cook for 5min, pour on the stock or water and simmer for 5min. Stir in the paprika pepper and add the fish. Cover the pan and simmer for a further 25min. Do not stir.

Smoked Haddock and Mushroom Pie*

2lb (1kg) smoked haddock
1lb (500g) mushrooms
1 tbsp (10g, 1¼ tbsp) chopped parsley
½pt (250ml, 1¼ cups) milk
1oz (25g, ¼ cup) flour
4oz (100g, ½ cup) butter

Preparation time: about 30min   Cooking time: 35min

Clean and finely slice the mushrooms. Put the haddock into a roasting tin, add water and 1oz (25g, 2tbsp) butter. Cook in a moderate oven, 400° F, 205° C, mark 6, for 10min. Drain, skin and remove any bones from the haddock and put the fish into a shallow casserole. Keep hot. Make a white sauce with 1oz (25g, 2tbsp) of the butter, milk and flour. Melt remaining butter and fry mushrooms. Pour the mushrooms and melted butter over the haddock, adding salt and pepper to taste. Sprinkle on the chopped parsley and pour the white sauce over the top. Cook in a moderate oven, 350° F, 180° C, mark 4, for 10min. Serve hot.

Smoked Haddock Puff

1lb (500g) smoked haddock
1lb (500g) potatoes
2oz (50g) chopped onions
2 eggs
1 tbsp (10g, 1¼ tbsp) chopped parsley
2oz (50g, 4 tbsp) butter
4 tbsp (65ml, ⅓ cup) milk

Preparation time: about 40min   Cooking time: 40min

Grease a 9in (23cm) soufflé dish. Peel the potatoes and cover with water in a large saucepan, add 1 tsp salt and boil for 20min. Put the haddock in a casserole, cover with water and cook for 10min. Drain the haddock, remove the skin and any bones. Drain and mash the potatoes, add the milk and beat well. Flake the fish with a fork and fold into the mashed potato. Add parsley and onion with salt and pepper to taste. Separate the egg yolks from the whites. Whisk the yolks and add to

44

the haddock and potato. Whisk the whites until stiff and fold into the haddock. Put the mixture into the prepared soufflé dish, dot with the butter and cook in a moderate oven, 350° F, 180° C, mark 4, for 20min.

Baked Scallops*

8 scallops
¾pt (375ml, 2 cups) milk
1½oz (40g, 6 tbsp) flour
6oz (150g) mushrooms
4oz (100g, ½ cup) butter
2oz (50g, ¾ cup) dried breadcrumbs

Preparation time: about 30min   Cooking time: 35min

Remove the scallops from their shells and put into cold water to clean thoroughly, then drain and cut them in halves. Put the scallops into a saucepan, pour over the milk and leave to simmer for 10min. Strain, keeping the milk and put the scallops into a casserole. Clean the mushrooms and slice finely. Melt 1½oz (40g, 3 tbsp) of butter and fry them for 5min. Put the mushrooms on top of the scallops. Make a white sauce (see page 13) with the strained milk, 1½oz (40g, 3 tbsp) of butter and the flour. Pour the sauce over the scallops and mushrooms, sprinkle with the breadcrumbs and dot with the remaining butter. Cook in a moderately hot oven, 400° F, 205° C, mark 6, for 10min.

Coquilles St Jacques Mornay*

4 scallops
1oz (25g) Gruyère cheese
4oz (100g) button mushrooms
2oz (50g) onions
½pt (250ml, 1¼ cups) white wine
1 bay leaf
1 tbsp (10g, 1¼ tbsp) chopped parsley
¼pt (125ml, scant ¾ cup) milk
1oz (25g, ¼ cup) flour
1oz (25g, 2 tbsp) butter
1oz (25g, ¼ cup) grated Parmesan cheese

Preparation time: about 30min   Cooking time: 30min

Grate the Gruyère cheese. Remove the scallops from their shells and clean them in cold water. Clean and finely slice the mushrooms. Peel and finely chop the onion. Put the scallops into a saucepan with the white wine, bay leaf and chopped parsley and add salt and pepper. Simmer for 10min. Strain, keeping the liquid. Cut the scallops into four and put them back into their shells. Keep hot. Melt the butter in a saucepan and cook the mushrooms and onion for 5min. Remove the pan from the heat and stir in the flour. When well blended, stir in the milk and strained white wine. Return the pan to the heat and cook over a low heat for 5min. Stir in the Gruyère and half the Parmesan cheese, then cook for a further 5min. Pour the sauce over the scallops, sprinkle on the rest of the Parmesan and put under a hot grill for 5min or until golden brown.

Scampi Meunière

1½pt (525g, 1lb 2oz) prawns
3oz (75g, ¾ cup) flour
4oz (100g, ½ cup) butter
4 tbsp (65ml, ⅓ cup) oil
2 tbsp (25ml, 2½ tbsp) lemon juice
1 tbsp (10g, 1¼ tbsp) chopped parsley
1 lemon

Preparation time: about 25min   Cooking time: 10min

Shell and clean the prawns. Toss the prawns in the seasoned flour. Heat the oil and half the butter in a frying pan, add the prawns and cook for 5min. Put the prawns on to a hot serving dish. Sprinkle with lemon juice. Melt the rest of the butter, add the parsley and stir well. Pour the melted butter over the prawns and serve hot with wedges of lemon.

Scampi Provençale*

1½pt (525g, 1lb 2oz) prawns
8oz (250g) tomatoes
2oz (50g) onions
4 tbsp (65ml, ⅓ cup) oil
2 garlic cloves
1 tbsp (10g, 1¼ tbsp) chopped parsley
1 tsp (5g, 1¼ tsp) sugar
2 tbsp (40ml, 2½ tbsp) tomato purée

Preparation time: about 30min   Cooking time: 25min

Skin and roughly chop the tomatoes. Peel and roughly chop the onion and garlic. Heat the oil and cook the onion and garlic for 5min. Add the tomatoes, tomato purée, parsley, sugar and salt and black pepper to taste. Simmer for 15min. While the tomatoes are cooking, shell and clean the prawns. Add them to the tomatoes and stirring, continue cooking for 5min. Serve hot with boiled rice (see page 102).

Prawn Newburg

1½pt (525g, 1lb 2oz) prawns
6oz (150g, ⅞ cup) long grain rice
2oz (50g, 4 tbsp) butter
¼pt (125ml, scant ¾ cup) sherry
2 egg yolks
¼pt (125ml, scant ¾ cup) single cream
1¼pt (625ml, 3¼ cups) water

Preparation time: about 30min   Cooking time: 20min

Bring the water to the boil, add 1 tsp salt and sprinkle in the rice. Bring to the boil again and simmer for 20min or until all the water has been absorbed by the rice. While the rice is cooking, shell and clean the prawns. Melt the butter in a large frying pan and cook the prawns for 5min over a low heat. Remove the pan from the heat and stir in the sherry. Cover and cook for a further 5min. Whisk the egg yolks, add salt and pepper to taste and stir in the cream. Remove the frying pan from the heat, stir the yolk and cream mixture into the prawns and cook over a low heat for 10min to allow the sauce to thicken. Serve hot with the rice.

Trout Armandine

4 trout
4oz (100g, scant 1 cup) blanched almonds
4oz (100g, 1 cup) flour
5oz (125g, 10 tbsp) butter
3 tbsp (30g, 3¾ tbsp) chopped parsley
2 tbsp (25ml, 2½ tbsp) lemon juice

Preparation time: about 20min   Cooking time: 15min
Clean the trout but do not remove the head or tail. Add salt and
pepper to the flour. Dip the trout in the seasoned flour. Melt 4oz
(100g, ½ cup) of butter in a frying pan and cook the trout on both
sides for about 10min. Remove the trout, put them on a hot serving
dish and keep hot. Clean the pan, melt the remaining butter, add the
almonds and cook until golden brown. Add the lemon juice and
chopped parsley. Pour the sauce over the trout.

Trout with Melted Butter

4 trout
½pt (250ml, 1¼ cups) white wine vinegar
1 lemon
4oz (100g, ½ cup) butter
4 tbsp (40g, 5 tbsp) chopped parsley
2 tbsp (25ml, 2½ tbsp) lemon juice

Preparation time: about 1hr and 20min   Cooking time: 25min
Slice the lemon finely. Clean the trout but do not remove the head or
tail. Heat the vinegar. Put the trout in a dish and pour on the heated
vinegar. Cover and leave for 1hr. Remove the fish, put them into a
large pan, cover with boiling water and cook over a low heat for
15min. Remove the fish from the water and place on a heated serving
dish. Garnish with slices of lemon and half the chopped parsley.
Melt the butter but do not brown. Stir in the lemon juice and the
rest of the chopped parsley. Pour the butter sauce over the trout.

Lemon Glazed Herrings

4 herrings
4 lemons
1 tbsp (10g, 1¼ tbsp) English dry mustard
3oz (75g, ¾ cup) brown sugar

Preparation time: about 50min   Cooking time: 20min
Clean the herrings. Slice 2 lemons. Grate the rind from the remaining lemons and squeeze out the juice. Mix the mustard and brown sugar with the lemon rind and juice. Add a pinch of salt. Rub half the mixture into the fish and leave for 30min. Cook the herrings under a hot grill for 10min, turning once. Put the lemon slices on top of the fish and grill for a further 5min. Heat the remaining sugar and lemon mixture and pour over herrings. Serve hot.

Sardine Rolls

Flaky pastry
8oz (250g, 2 cups) plain flour
6oz (150g, ¾ cup) butter
½ tbsp (7ml, ¾ tbsp) lemon juice
Filling
15oz (375g) tinned sardines
2oz (50g) tomatoes
4oz (100g) black olives
1 egg

Preparation time: about 1hr and 45min   Cooking time: 20min
Make the flaky pastry (see page 11). Drain the sardines and split in half, remove the backbone. Cut the olives in half and remove the stones. Skin and finely slice the tomatoes. Cut the pastry into 8 oblong shapes, 3in (7¾cm) by 4in (10¼cm). Put a slice of tomato on one half of each sardine, top with olives and sprinkle with salt and pepper. Place the other halves of the sardines on top. Put a stuffed sardine on each oblong of pastry, dampen the edges and fold over. Crimp the edges with a fork. Make two slits in the pastry. Whisk the egg and brush over the rolls. Put them on to a greased baking sheet and bake in a moderately hot oven, 400° F, 205° C, mark 6, for 20min. Serve hot or cold.

Salmon Quiches*

Shortcrust pastry
8oz (250g, 2 cups) flour
4oz (100g, ½ cup) fat
Filling
8oz (250g) tinned pink salmon
2oz (50g) onions
1 egg
¼pt (125ml, scant ¾ cup) double cream
2oz (50g, 4 tbsp) butter
1 tbsp (10g, 1¼ tbsp) chopped parsley

Preparation time: about 45min   Cooking time: 30min
Grease and flour four 4in (10cm) patty tins. Make the shortcrust pastry (see page 11). Line the patty tins, put a disc of greaseproof paper in each tin, top with dried beans and bake blind in a moderately hot oven, 400° F, 205° C, mark 6, for 10min. Remove the greaseproof and beans. Peel and finely chop the onion. Beat the salmon until soft. Whisk the egg and cream together. Melt the butter and cook the onion for 5min. Remove from the heat. Fold the onion into the salmon, add the egg and cream and chopped parsley. Stir well. Add salt and pepper to taste. Fill the patty cases with the mixture, sprinkle with paprika pepper and cook in a moderate oven, 350° F, 180°C, mark 4, for 15min. Serve hot or cold.

Fried Whitebait

1lb (500g) whitebait
6oz (150g, 1½ cups) flour
2 lemons

Preparation time: about 20min   Cooking time: 15min
Rinse the whitebait in cold water and dry thoroughly on kitchen paper. Add salt and pepper to the flour and shake the whitebait in it. Heat some oil in a deep frying pan, put some of the whitebait in the wire basket and fry for 3min. When the whitebait is crisp, drain on kitchen paper, then put on to a hot serving plate and keep hot while cooking the rest of the fish. Sprinkle with salt and pepper and serve hot with wedges of lemon.

Shrimp Pie*

Shortcrust pastry
8oz (250g, 2 cups) flour
4oz (100g, ½ cup) fat
Filling
1pt (350g, ¾lb) shrimps
2oz (50g) onion
4oz (100g) mushrooms
1 tbsp (15ml, 1¼ tbsp) Worcestershire sauce
2oz (50g, 4 tbsp) butter
¼pt (125ml, scant ¾ cup) single cream
2 eggs

Preparation time: about 45min   Cooking time: 35min
Grease and flour a 9in (23cm) flan tin. Make the shortcrust pastry (see page 11) and line the tin. Peel the onion and chop finely. Clean the mushrooms and slice. Shell and clean the shrimps. Melt the butter then cook the onion and mushrooms for 5min. Add the shrimps with salt and pepper to taste. Put the shrimps, onions and mushrooms into the prepared flan case. Whisk the eggs, add the cream and Worcestershire sauce, mix well and pour over the shrimps. Cook in a moderately hot oven, 400° F, 205° C, mark 6, for 30min. Serve either hot or cold.

Sole Veronique

2lb (1kg) sole fillets
½pt (250ml, 1¼ cups) white wine
½pt (250ml, 1¼ cups) fish stock
1½oz (40g, 3 tbsp) butter
1½oz (40g, ¾ cup) flour
8oz (250g) white grapes
¼pt (125ml, scant ¾ cup) single cream

Preparation time: about 40min   Cooking time: 25min
Skin the grapes, cut in half and remove pips. Remove the skins from the fillets of sole and sprinkle with salt and pepper. Put the sole into a large frying pan and pour over the white wine and fish stock. Cook over a low heat for 10min. Take the fish from the pan and put on to

a hot serving dish to keep hot. Strain the stock. Melt the butter in a saucepan, remove the pan from the heat and stir in the flour. When blended, gradually add the strained stock and stir well. Replace the saucepan on the heat and, stirring, allow the sauce to boil, then cook for a couple of minutes. Remove the pan from the heat and stir in the cream and grapes. Reheat and pour the sauce over the sole.

MEAT

Beef Olives*

1lb (500g) fillet beef
8oz (250g) onions
8oz (250g) carrots
3oz (75g, 6 tbsp) dripping
1½pt (750ml, 3¼ cups) stock
Filling
2oz (50g, ½ cup) suet
2oz (50g, 1½ cups) white breadcrumbs
1 tsp (5g, 1¼ tsp) mixed herbs
1 tbsp (10g, 1¼ tbsp) chopped parsley
1 egg

Preparation time: about 40min Cooking time: 1¾hr
Finely chop the suet and mix together with the breadcrumbs, mixed herbs, chopped parsley and salt and pepper to taste. Whisk the egg and stir into the suet mixture. Finely slice the beef and cut into 3in (8¾cm) squares. Flatten the beef squares with a meat tenderiser or wooden rolling pin. Place some of the filling on each square and roll up, securing the rolls with white thread.

Peel and finely slice the onions and carrots. Melt half the dripping in a frying pan and fry the onions until soft. Remove onions from the pan and put them into a casserole. Put the sliced carrots on top of the onions. Melt the rest of the dripping and brown the beef olives, then put on top of the carrots. Pour the stock over the top and cook in a very low oven, 300° F, 180° C, mark 2, for 1½hr. When cooked, remove the beef olives from the casserole and carefully remove the thread from each olive, replace them in the casserole and serve with mashed potato.

Beef in Soya Sauce*

1lb (500g) beef
4oz (100g) onions
4oz (100g, ½ cup) butter
3 tbsp (50ml, 4 tbsp) soya sauce
2 tbsp (25ml, 2½ tbsp) vinegar
1oz (25g, ¼ cup) soft brown sugar
½pt (250ml, 1¼ cups) water
1 tsp (5g, 1¼ tsp) ground nutmeg

Preparation time: about 30min   Cooking time: 40min
Cut the meat into narrow strips 1½in (4cm) long. Peel and slice the
onions. Melt half the butter and fry the onions until soft. Put the
soya sauce, vinegar, brown sugar and remaining butter in a casserole
and heat, stirring all the time. Add the strips of meat and simmer
gently for 5min. Add the onion to the meat and ground nutmeg, pour
in the water and stir gently. Simmer the meat over a low heat for
30min. Serve with plain boiled rice.

Boeuf Stroganov*

1lb (500g) fillet beef
4oz (100g) onions
3oz (75g, ¾ cup) flour
¼ pint (125ml, scant ¾ cup) sour cream
3oz (75g, 6 tbsp) butter
½pt (250ml, 1¼ cups) meat stock

Preparation time: about 30min   Cooking time: 35min
Peel and finely chop the onions. Add salt and pepper to the flour
and stir well. Cut the beef into thin slices, flatten them with a meat
tenderiser or wooden rolling pin. Cut the beef into thin strips 1½in
(4cm) long. Dip the strips of beef in the flour to coat them lightly.
Melt the butter and lightly brown the strips of beef, remove the meat
from the pan and keep hot. Fry the onions in the butter until soft.
Return the meat to the pan, add the stock and simmer over a low heat
for 25min. Stir in the sour cream just before serving.

Gulyas (Hungarian Stew)*

2lb (1kg) beef
4oz (100g, ½ cup) dripping
8oz (250g) onions
8oz (250g) tomatoes
1lb (500g) potatoes
½ tbsp (5g, ¾ tbsp) paprika pepper
1oz (25g, 2 tbsp) butter
1¾pt (1l, 2 cups) water
2 tbsp (40ml, 2½ tbsp) tomato purée

Preparation time: about 40min   Cooking time: 3hr and 10min

Cut the meat into cubes about 3in (8¾cm) square. Peel and finely chop the onions. Skin and chop the tomatoes. Melt the dripping in a large casserole and fry the onion until soft, add the beef and, stirring, cook until browned. Add salt, half the paprika pepper and stir in the tomatoes. Mix the tomato purée with half the water and pour over the meat, then simmer gently for 2hr. Peel the potatoes, cut them into thick slices and put on top of the meat. Melt the butter, stir in the paprika pepper and stir into the stew. Pour over the remaining water and continue simmering for another hour. Serve hot.

Lamb Cooked in Yogurt

4 thick lamb chops
4oz (100g, ½ cup) butter
½pt (250ml, 1¼ cups) natural yogurt
1pt (500ml, 2½ cups) stock

Preparation time: about 20min   Cooking time: 1hr and 20min

Trim the chops. Melt the butter in a casserole and brown the chops on both sides. Pour the stock into the casserole, add salt and pepper and cook in a low oven, 325° F, 165° C, mark 3, for 1hr. Remove the casserole from the oven and pour in the yogurt. Continue cooking for a further 10min. Serve with rice.

Lamb Cutlets Milanaise Style

8 lamb cutlets
2 eggs
4oz (100g, 1½ cups) browned fine breadcrumbs
2oz (50g, 4 tbsp) butter
2 tbsp (25ml, 2½ tbsp) olive oil

Preparation time: about 20min   Cooking time: 15min

Whisk the eggs, adding salt and pepper. Trim the cutlets and flatten with a meat tenderiser. Dip the cutlets into the eggs and then into the breadcrumbs. Heat the butter and olive oil in a frying pan and fry the cutlets for 15min, turning once. Serve with wedges of lemon and parsley.

Stuffed Lamb

3lb (1·500kg) boned shoulder lamb
6oz (150g, 2¼ cups) white breadcrumbs
15oz (475g, 2 cups) crushed pineapple
3oz (75g, ¾ cup) brown sugar
2oz (50g) onions
2 tbsp (25ml, 2½ tbsp) lemon juice
2oz (50g, ½ cup) chopped walnuts
2oz (50g, 4 tbsp) butter
1 tsp (3g, 1¼ tsp) ginger
3 tbsp (50ml, 4 tbsp) soya sauce
2oz (50g, 4 tbsp) dripping
1 garlic clove

Preparation time: about 1½hr   Cooking time: 1½hr

Peel and finely chop the onions. Peel and crush the garlic. Melt the butter and fry the breadcrumbs until browned. Remove the pan from the heat and stir in the crushed pineapple, brown sugar, onion, chopped walnuts, ginger and garlic. Leave for 1hr. Pre-heat the oven to 350° F, 180° C, mark 4. Brush the inside of the lamb with the lemon juice, fill with the stuffing, roll and tie securely with string. Melt the dripping in a roasting pan and put in the lamb. Pour over the soya sauce and cover. Cook for 1½hr basting frequently.

Lamb Cutlets in Red Wine*

8 lamb cutlets
¾pt (375ml, 2 cups) red wine
2oz (50g) onions
1oz (25g, ¼ cup) stuffed olives
2oz (50g, 4 tbsp) butter

Preparation time: about 1hr   Cooking time: 55min
Trim the cutlets. Peel and finely slice the onion. Slice the olives.
Melt the butter and brown the cutlets on each side. Cover the cutlets
with the onion and olives. Sprinkle with oregano, paprika pepper and
salt and pepper. Pour over the red wine and leave for 1hr, then cook
in a slow oven, 325° F, 165° C, mark 3, for 45min. Serve hot with
mashed potato.

Chilli con Carne

1lb (500g, 2 cups) minced meat
8oz (250g, 1½ cups) dried red kidney beans
4oz (100g) onions
1 tbsp (10g, 1¼ tbsp) chilli powder
1 garlic clove
3oz (75g, 6 tbsp) dripping
8oz (250g) tomatoes

Preparation time: overnight and about 30min   Cooking time: 3½hr
Soak the red kidney beans overnight in a large bowl of cold water.
Next day, drain the beans and put them into a large saucepan. Cover
with water and bring to the boil, then simmer for 2hr. Drain, keeping
the liquid. Skin and chop the tomatoes. Peel and finely chop the
onions. Peel and crush the garlic. Melt the dripping in a large saucepan
and fry the onion until soft. Add the meat and garlic and cook for a
further 5min. Add the drained beans to the meat and stir in the tomatoes,
chilli powder and salt to taste. Pour ¾pt (375ml) of the strained liquid
into the saucepan and stir well. Cover and simmer over a low heat
for 1hr and 20min.

Lancashire Hot-pot*

2lb (1kg) best end neck of lamb
4oz (100g) onions
1½lb (750g) potatoes
2 sheep's kidneys
1pt (500ml, 2½ cups) water
2oz (50g, 4 tbsp) dripping

Preparation time: about 35min   Cooking time: 2½hr

Trim the meat and cut into cutlets. Remove any surplus fat. Slice the kidneys. Peel the onions and cut into halves. Put with meat trimmings, fat and water, in a saucepan, bring to the boil and simmer for 30min. Strain the liquid. Peel and slice the potatoes. Melt half the dripping in a casserole. Arrange half the potatoes in a layer in the casserole, then a layer of cutlets, then the sliced kidneys and lastly the remaining potatoes. Add salt and pepper. Melt the remaining dripping and brush over the potatoes then pour over the stock. Cover and cook in a moderate oven, 350° F, 180° C, mark 4, for 1½hr. Remove the cover from the casserole and cook for a further 30min.

Minced Meat Crumble*

1½lb (750g, 3 cups) minced meat
8oz (250g) onions
2 tbsp (40ml, 2½ tbsp) tomato purée
2oz (50g, 4 tbsp) dripping
4oz (100g, 1 cup) flour
2oz (50g, 4 tbsp) butter
¼pt (125ml, scant ¾ cup) water

Preparation time: about 35min   Cooking time: 45min
Peel and finely chop the onion then fry in melted dripping until soft.
Add the minced meat and salt and pepper to taste. Stirring, cook for
10min. Add the tomato purée to the meat and pour in the water.
Continue cooking, stirring for a further 5min. Put the meat into a
casserole. Sift the flour into a large bowl, add a pinch of salt and, using
the fingertips, rub the butter into the flour until the mixture resembles
fine breadcrumbs. Put the crumble mixture on to the top of the
meat and cook in a moderate oven, 350° F, 180° C, mark 4, for 25min.
Serve hot.

Pork Chops in Orange Sauce

4 pork chops
3oz (75g) onions
4oz (100g, 1 cup) brown sugar
1 tsp (3g, 1¼ tsp) ginger
3oz (75g, 6 tbsp) butter
½pt (250ml, 1¼ cups) orange juice
1 tbsp (15ml, 1¼ tbsp) lemon juice
¼pt (125ml, scant ¾ cup) water

Preparation time: about 35min   Cooking time: 1½hr
Trim the chops. Peel and finely chop the onions. Melt the butter in
a large frying pan and brown the chops on either side. Remove and
put into a casserole. Fry the onions in the butter until soft. Remove
the pan from the heat and stir in the brown sugar, ginger, orange juice,
lemon juice and water. Add a pinch of salt and stir well. Pour the
sauce over the chops and cook in a moderate oven, 350° F, 180° C,
mark 4, for 1¼hr.

Sweet and Sour Pork

1lb (500g) pork
2 eggs
2oz (50g, ½ cup) flour
½pt (250ml, 1¼ cups) oil for frying
Sauce
1 tbsp (15ml, 1¼ tbsp) soya sauce
1oz (25g, scant ⅓ cup) cornflour
2 tbsp (25ml, 2½ tbsp) vinegar
1oz (25g, ¼ cup) brown sugar
1 red pepper
½pt (250ml, 1¼ cups) pineapple juice
4oz (100g) young carrots
3 tbsp (50ml, 4 tbsp) olive oil

Preparation time: about 45min   Cooking time: 20min

Make the sweet and sour sauce (see page 14). Cut the pork into 1in (2½cm) cubes. Whisk the eggs and add the flour with a large pinch of salt, stir well. Dip the pieces of pork into the egg mixture. Heat the oil until very hot and drop in the pork. Fry until crisp, for about 5min. Put the pork into the sweet and sour sauce and cook over a low heat for 5min. Serve hot.

Gammon Steaks Cooked in Foil

1lb (500g) gammon steaks
15oz (475g, 2 cups) pineapple slices
2oz (50g, 4 tbsp) butter
½oz (15g, 1¼ tbsp) cloves

Preparation time: about 30min   Cooking time: 40min

Trim the gammon and cut into 4 equal steaks. Drain the pineapple. Cut 4 pieces of foil large enough to enclose the gammon steaks. Put a gammon steak on each piece of foil, cover with two slices of pineapple. Dot the gammon steaks with the butter, stick four cloves into each piece of pineapple and sprinkle with paprika pepper. Fold the foil tightly over the gammon steaks and put on to a baking sheet. Cook in a moderate oven, 350° F, 180° C, mark 4, for 40min. Serve hot in the foil.

Pork Chops in Red Wine

4 pork chops
½pt (250ml, 1¼ cups) red wine
1 lemon
4oz (100g, ½ cup) butter

Preparation time: about 1hr　　　　　　　　　Cooking time: 1hr

Squeeze the juice from the lemon. Trim the chops, removing any surplus fat, then rub with salt, pepper and lemon juice. Leave for 30min. Melt the butter, brown the chops on both sides and put them into a shallow casserole with the butter. Cook for 30min in a moderate oven, 350° F, 180° C, mark 4. Pour the red wine over the chops and simmer until tender—about 20min. Serve with rice and the red wine sauce.

Bacon Rolls with Cream Cheese

8oz (250g) back bacon rashers
8oz (250g) prunes
4oz (100g, ½ cup) cream cheese
¼pt (125ml, scant ¾ cup) sour cream
2oz (50g) onions
2oz (50g, 4 tbsp) butter

Preparation time: about 45min   Cooking time: 50min

Put the prunes in a saucepan, cover with water and simmer for 20min. Drain the prunes and remove the stones. Peel and finely chop the onion. Mix the onion and cream cheese together, add salt and pepper to taste. Remove the rinds from the bacon. Put two prunes and a spoonful of cream cheese at one end of each bacon rasher, roll up and secure with a wooden cocktail stick. Put the bacon rolls into a greased dish, dot with butter and cook in a moderately low oven, 325° F, 165° C, mark 3, for 30min. Remove the dish from the oven and pour on the sour cream. Serve immediately.

Baked Spiced Gammon with Cheese

1lb (500g) gammon slices
2oz (50g) onions
1 tbsp (20ml, 1¼ tbsp) tomato purée
1 tsp (3g, 1¼ tsp) ground cloves
2oz (50g, 1½ cups) white breadcrumbs
2oz (50g) Cheddar cheese
½pt (250ml, 1¼ cups) water

Preparation time: about 30min   Cooking time: 35min

Peel and finely chop the onions. Grate the cheese. Mix together the onion, tomato purée, ground cloves, water and a pinch of pepper. Put the gammon into a shallow dish and pour over the sauce, cook in a moderately hot oven, 375° F, 190° C, mark 5, for 30min. Remove from the oven. Mix together the breadcrumbs and cheese and sprinkle over the gammon. Put the gammon under a hot grill for 5min. Serve hot.

Gammon Steaks in Red Wine

1lb (500g) gammon steaks
15oz (475g, 2 cups) tinned cherries
1pt (500ml, 2½ cups) red wine
2 bay leaves

Preparation time: about 30min   Cooking time: 45min

Trim the fat from the gammon and cut into 4 equal steaks. Drain the cherries and remove the stones. Put the steaks into a shallow dish, cover with the cherries, bay leaves and a pinch of pepper. Pour the red wine over the gammon and cover the dish with foil. Cook in a moderate oven, 350° F, 180° C, mark 4, for 45min. Serve hot.

Ham Rolls with Apricots

8oz (250g) ham
8oz (250g, 1 full cup) dried apricots
4 tbsp (65ml, ⅓ cup) mango chutney
½oz (12g, 2 tbsp) cornflour or flour
2oz (50g, ¼ cup) granulated sugar
1 lemon
1pt (500ml, 2½ cups) water
2oz (50g, 4 tbsp) butter

Preparation time: overnight and about 40min   Cooking time: 45min

Put the apricots into a bowl, cover with water and leave to soak overnight. Next day, peel the rind from the lemon, squeeze out the juice and put rind and juice into a saucepan. Add apricots, water and sugar. Cook over a low heat for 30min, topping up the liquid if necessary. Drain the apricots, keeping the juice. Spread the mango chutney over the slices of ham. Put the apricots on the slices and roll the ham up, securing each slice with a wooden cocktail stick. Put the ham rolls into a greased shallow dish, dot with butter and cook in a moderate oven, 350° F, 180° C, mark 4, for 15min. While the ham rolls are cooking, blend the cornflour or flour with a little water, when smooth, stir in the apricot juice and simmer over a low heat until the sauce thickens. Serve the sauce hot with the ham rolls.

64

Pineapple and Ham Casserole

1lb (500g) ham
15oz (475g, 2 cups) tinned pineapple pieces
1oz (25g, ¼ cup) cornflour or flour
15oz (475g, 2 cups) tinned tomatoes
1lb (500g) potatoes

Preparation time: about 35min   Cooking time: 40min

Roughly chop the ham. Drain the pineapple pieces, keeping the juice. Peel the potatoes and cook for 10min, then drain and slice. Drain the tomatoes, keeping the juice. Put the ham, pineapple pieces, tomatoes and potatoes in layers in a casserole. Put the cornflour or flour in a bowl. Heat the pineapple and tomato juices and stir into the cornflour or flour. When blended, pour the sauce over the ham. Cook in a moderate oven, 350° F, 180° C, mark 4, for 25min. Serve hot.

Italian Stuffed Pancakes

Batter
½pt (250ml, 1¼ cups) milk
4oz (100g, ½ cup) flour
1 egg
Sauce
2oz (50g, 4 tbsp) butter
1oz (25g, ¼ cup) flour
½pt (250ml, 1¼ cups) milk
¼pt (125ml, scant ¾ cup) double cream
Filling
8oz (250g) ham
2 eggs
2oz (50g) Mozzarella cheese
1oz (25g, ¼ cup) grated Parmesan cheese
1 tsp (3g, 1¼ tsp) dry mustard
1 tsp (3g, 1¼ tsp) oregano

Preparation time: about 1¼hr   Cooking time: 1hr

Make the batter (see page 12) and a white sauce (see page 13). Stir the cream into the white sauce after cooking. Heat some fat in a

E   65

frying pan and pour in a little of the batter. Cook the pancake until it is light brown on one side, loosen the edges and turn, cooking on the other side until light brown. Keep hot on a dish and, using all the batter, make another seven pancakes.

Whisk the eggs. Finely chop the ham and Mozzarella cheese. Mix together half the sauce, eggs, ham, Mozzarella cheese, mustard and half the Parmesan cheese. Sprinkle in a pinch of nutmeg, salt and pepper and mix well. Put 2 tbsp of filling in the centre of each pancake and roll up. Pour the rest of the sauce into a shallow casserole and lay the stuffed pancakes on top. Sprinkle with the remaining Parmesan cheese. Cook in a moderate oven, 350° F, 180° C, mark 4, for 25min. Serve hot.

Scalloped Ham*

12oz (350g) ham
1lb (500g) potatoes
1 green pepper
2oz (50g) onions
3oz (75g, 6 tbsp) butter
3oz (75g) cheese
½pt (250ml, 1¼ cups) milk
1oz (25g, ¼ cup) flour

Preparation time: about 40min   Cooking time: 40min
Peel and cook the potatoes in boiling salted water for 20min. Remove the stalk, core and seeds from the green pepper. Peel and finely chop the onion. Chop the pepper and ham. Grate the cheese. Make a white sauce with the milk, flour and 1oz (25g, 2 tbsp) of butter. Melt 1oz (25g, 2 tbsp) of butter and cook the onion and pepper until soft, add the ham and cook for a further 5min. Stir the onion, pepper and ham into the white sauce, add salt and pepper to taste. Put the ham mixture into a greased shallow casserole and keep hot.

Drain the potatoes and mash thoroughly. Beat in the remaining butter and pipe the potatoes round the edge of the ham. Sprinkle the cheese on top and cook in a moderate oven, 350° F, 180° C, mark 4, for 15min. Serve hot.

Quiche Lorraine*

Shortcrust pastry
8oz (250g, 2 cups) flour
4oz (100g, ½ cup) fat
Filling
4oz (100g) streaky bacon
2 eggs
¼pt (125ml, scant ¾ cup) single cream
2oz (50g, 4 tbsp) butter
¼pt (125ml, scant ¾ cup) milk

Preparation time: about 45min   Cooking time: 35min

Make the shortcrust pastry (see page 11). Roll out and line an 8in (20cm) flan tin. De-rind the bacon and chop it into small pieces then fry until crisp in half the melted butter, and scatter over the pastry. Whisk the eggs and mix together with the milk and cream, salt and pepper. Pour the eggs over the bacon. Dot with the remaining butter. Bake in a moderately hot oven, 400° F, 205° C, mark 6, for 20min, then reduce the heat to 350° F, 180° C, mark 4 and cook for a further 10min. Serve hot or cold.

Savoury Meat Roll*

Filling
1lb (500g) sausage meat
4oz (100g) onions
1 green pepper
1oz (25g, ¼ cup) pine nuts
1 egg
Shortcrust pastry
8oz (250g, 2 cups) plain flour
4oz (100g, ½ cup) fat

Preparation time: about 45min   Cooking time: 45min

Make the shortcrust pastry (see page 11), roll out into a large square and neaten the edges. Peel and finely chop the onions. Remove the core and seeds from the pepper and chop it finely. Mix together the sausage meat, onions, pepper and pine nuts, salt and pepper to taste. Put the sausage meat on one half of the pastry, dampen the edges and fold over. Crimp the edges of the pastry together, cut four slits in the top and put the meat roll on to a greased baking sheet. Whisk the egg and brush the egg over the pastry. Bake in a hot oven, 425° F, 220° C, mark 7, for 10min, then reduce the heat to 350° F, 180°C, mark 4, for 35min. Serve hot or cold in slices.

Sausage, Apple and Onion Layer

1lb (500g) sausage meat
4oz (100g) onions
1lb (500g) cooking apples
15oz (475g, 2 cups) tinned tomatoes
2oz (50g, 4 tbsp) butter

Preparation time: about 45min   Cooking time: 45min
Peel and finely slice the onions. Add salt and pepper to the sausage meat and mix well. Peel, core and slice the apples. Lay the apple slices on the bottom of a greased casserole, put the sausage meat on top, then the onion slices and lastly the tomatoes and their juice. Dot with butter and sprinkle with thyme. Bake in a moderately hot oven, 375° F, 190° C, mark 5, for 45min. Serve hot.

Sausage Casserole

1lb (500g) skinless sausages
11½oz (326g, 1¼ cups) tinned corn kernels
1lb (500g) bananas
Batter
1 egg
½pt (250ml, 1¼ cups) milk
4oz (100g, 1 cup) flour

Preparation time: about 40min   Cooking time: 1hr and 10min
Make a batter (see page 12). Put the drained corn into a greased casserole. Fry the sausages in their own fat. Peel the bananas and put the sausages and bananas on top of the corn. Pour over the batter and cook in a hot oven, 450° F, 230° C, mark 8, for 1hr. Serve hot.

Sausage and Vegetable Casserole

1lb (500g) sausages
2oz (50g) onions
8oz (250g) carrots
8oz (250g) streaky bacon
14oz (396g, 1¾ cups) tinned tomatoes
8oz (250g) mushrooms
1oz (25g, 2 tbsp) sugar
1oz (25g, 2 tbsp) dripping

Preparation time: about 40min   Cooking time: 1¼hr
Peel and slice the onions and carrots. Clean and slice the mushrooms. Melt the dripping and brown the sausages on all sides. Remove the sausages from the pan and wrap half a rasher of bacon round each one. Fry the onions and mushrooms in the dripping until soft. Put the sausages in a casserole, and top with the carrots, onions and mushrooms. Strain the tomatoes and put them into the casserole. Mix the tomato juice with the sugar, adding salt and pepper and a pinch of oregano. Pour the sauce over the sausages and vegetables, cover and cook in a moderate oven, 350° F, 180° C, mark 4, for 1hr. Serve hot.

Meat Balls*

1lb (500g) veal
4oz (100g, 3 cups) soft breadcrumbs
4 tbsp (40g, 5 tbsp) chopped parsley
1 egg
4oz (100g, ½ cup) butter
4oz (100g, 1 cup) flour

Preparation time: about 40min   Cooking time: 20min
Mince the veal twice. Whisk the egg. Mix together the veal, breadcrumbs, chopped parsley, egg and salt and pepper. Form into small balls the size of a walnut and roll in the flour. Melt the butter in a frying pan and, stirring, fry the meat balls for 20min. Serve hot with tomato sauce (see page 15).

Devilled Kidneys

1lb (500g) kidneys
2oz (50g, 4 tbsp) butter
1oz (25g, ¼ cup) flour
1 tsp (3g, 1¼ tsp) curry powder
1 tsp (3g, 1¼ tsp) dry mustard
1 tsp (3g, 1¼ tsp) paprika pepper
1 tsp (3g, 1¼ tsp) salt
1 tsp (3g, 1¼ tsp) pepper
¼pt (125ml, scant ¾ cup) water

Preparation time: about 30min   Cooking time: 20min

Remove the fat and skin from the kidneys, rinse them in cold water and remove the centre cores. Mix together the curry powder, dry mustard, paprika pepper, salt and pepper, and blend in the water. Toss the kidneys in the flour. Melt the butter and cook the kidneys for 10min over a low heat. Pour over the spiced liquid and continue cooking for a further 10min. Serve with rice or on hot buttered toast.

Kidney Stuffed Onions*

4 large onions
4 kidneys
4oz (100g) mushrooms
1pt (500ml, 2½ cups) stock

Preparation time: about 30min   Cooking time: 1¼hr

Remove the outer skin from the onions and put them into a casserole.
Cover with water and simmer for 15min. Remove the fat and skin
from the kidneys, rinse in cold water and remove the centre core.
Clean and finely chop the mushrooms. Drain the onions and carefully
cut the tops off them. Remove the centres from the onions and chop
finely. Mix together the chopped mushrooms and chopped onions,
adding salt and pepper to taste. Put a kidney and some mushroom
mixture into each onion, replace the tops and put into a casserole.
Pour on the stock and cover with foil. Cook in a moderate oven,
350° F, 180° C, mark 4, for 1hr. Serve hot with cooked rice.

Liver Italian Style

1lb (500g) liver
2oz (50g, ½ cup) grated Parmesan cheese
1 egg
4oz (100g) Mozzarella cheese
2oz (50g, ¾ cup) dried breadcrumbs
3 tbsp (60ml, 4 tbsp) tomato purée
1 tbsp (10g, 1¼ tbsp) chopped parsley
2oz (50g, 4 tbsp) butter
2 tbsp (25ml, 2½ tbsp) oil
3 tbsp (50ml, 4 tbsp) water

Preparation time: about 30min   Cooking time: 40min

Whisk the egg. Mix together the Parmesan cheese, breadcrumbs and
a pinch of salt and pepper. Slice the liver and dip the slices into the
the egg, then into the cheese and breadcrumbs. Heat the butter and
oil and fry the liver on both sides for 3min. Drain on kitchen paper.
Slice the Mozzarella cheese and put the liver slices and cheese in
layers in a casserole. Mix the water into the tomato purée, stir in the
parsley and salt and pepper to taste, pour over the liver and cook in
a moderate oven, 350° F, 180° C, mark 4, for 30min. Serve hot.

Chicken Armandine

4 chicken joints
¾pt (375ml, 2 cups) chicken stock
1oz (25g, 2 tbsp) butter
2oz (50g, scant ½ cup) split almonds
2oz (50g, full ½ cup) cornflour
½ tsp (3g, ¾ tsp) dry mustard
4 tbsp (65ml, ⅓ cup) sherry
2oz (50g, ⅓ cup) brown sugar

Preparation time: about 30min　　　　　　　Cooking time: 55min

Brush the chicken joints with oil and put into a casserole. Pour over the stock and cook in a moderately hot oven, 375° F, 190° C, mark 5, for 40min. Remove the chicken from the casserole and keep hot on a serving dish. Mix together the cornflour, dry mustard and brown sugar. Blend in the sherry and a little of the hot stock. When well blended, pour into the stock, and, stirring, allow to thicken over a low heat. Melt the butter and, stirring constantly, fry the almonds until golden brown. Pour the sauce over the chicken and sprinkle the almonds over the top.

Chicken Curry

2lb (1kg) chicken
6oz (150g) onions
1 garlic clove
1 tbsp (10g, 1¼ tbsp) curry powder
1oz (25g, 2 tbsp) butter
1 tbsp (15ml, 1¼ tbsp) olive oil
1 bouquet garni

Preparation time: about 35min　　　　　　　Cooking time: 2½hr

Peel 2oz (50g) of the onions and cut in half. Put the chicken into a large saucepan, add the onion, a bouquet garni and salt and pepper. Cover with cold water and simmer for 2hr. Remove the chicken from the saucepan, strain and keep the stock. Remove all the meat from the chicken and slice finely.

Peel and finely slice the remaining onions. Peel and crush the garlic.

72

Melt the butter and oil and fry the onion and garlic until soft. Remove the pan from the heat and stir in the curry powder. Add ¾pt (375ml, 2 cups) of the chicken stock and the sliced chicken, stir well, replace the pan on the heat and simmer for 20min.

Serve the curry hot with plain boiled rice and lentil soup.

Suggestions for side dishes: Grated coconut, chutney, sliced bananas, poppadums (fried and broken into bits over the top of the curry), and Bombay duck.

Chicken Joints with Pineapple

4 chicken joints
15oz (475g, 2 cups) crushed pineapple
½ gill (60ml, ¼ cup) lemon juice
½ gill (60ml, ¼ cup) thin honey
2 tbsp (25ml, 2½ tbsp) soya sauce
1 tsp (3g, 1¼ tsp) ground ginger
½ gill (60ml, ¼ cup) oil

Preparation time: about 30min   Cooking time: 1hr

Rub the chicken joints with salt and pepper. Heat the oil and fry the chicken for 15min, turning frequently. Mix together the crushed pineapple, lemon juice, thin honey, soya sauce and ground ginger. Put the chicken joints into a casserole with the oil, cover with the pineapple mixture and cook in a moderate oven, 350° F, 180° C, mark 4, for 45min. Serve hot.

Chicken Livers with Almonds

1lb (500g) chicken livers
4oz (100g, ½ cup) long grain rice
4oz (100g) mushrooms
2oz (50g, 4 tbsp) butter
2oz (50g, scant ⅓ cup) split almonds
1oz (25g, ¼ cup) flour
½pt (250ml, 1¼ cups) white wine
¼pt (125ml, scant ¾ cup) milk
½pt (250ml, 1¼ cups) water

73

Preparation time: about 40min   Cooking time: 40min
Clean and slice the mushrooms. Bring the water to the boil, add 1 tsp
salt and sprinkle in the rice. Bring to the boil again, then lower the
heat and simmer for 20min, or until all the water has been absorbed.
Keep hot. While the rice is cooking, melt the butter in a frying pan
and cook the chicken livers for 5min. Add the mushrooms and continue cooking for a further 5min. Keep hot. Blend the flour with the
milk, add salt and pepper, and stir into the chicken and mushrooms.
Pour in the white wine and stirring, cook over a very low heat until
the sauce has thickened. Mix the livers and rice together and put into
a shallow casserole. Cover with the split almonds and cook in a
moderate oven, 325° F, 165° C, mark 3, for 20min. Serve hot.

Chicken Mayonnaise

2lb (1kg) boiling chicken
2oz (50g) onions
1 red pepper
2oz (50g, $\frac{1}{2}$ cup) black olives
1 lettuce
1oz (25g) anchovy fillets
1 bouquet garni
Mayonnaise
2 egg yolks
$\frac{1}{2}$pt (250ml, 1$\frac{1}{4}$ cups) olive oil
$\frac{1}{2}$ tsp (3g, $\frac{3}{4}$ tsp) salt
$\frac{1}{2}$ tsp (3g, $\frac{3}{4}$ tsp) dry mustard
1 tbsp (15ml, 1$\frac{1}{4}$ tbsp) lemon juice or wine vinegar

Preparation time: about 40min   Cooking time: 2hr
Peel and cut the onions in half. Put the chicken, onions, bouquet
garni and salt and pepper in a large saucepan. Cover with water and
simmer for 2hr. While the chicken is cooking, make the mayonnaise
(see page 13). Drain the anchovies. Cut the olives in half and remove
the stones. Remove the core and seeds from the red pepper and finely
slice. Remove the chicken from the stock and leave to go cold.
Shred the lettuce. Cut the meat from the chicken and put the chicken
meat on to a bed of shredded lettuce. Cover the chicken with the
mayonnaise and garnish with the olives, anchovies and red pepper.

Chicken Piri-Piri

4 chicken joints
2 chilli peppers
¼pt (125ml, scant ¾ cup) olive oil
2 bay leaves
1 lemon

Preparation time: about 4½hr   Cooking time: 40min

Cut the chilli peppers in half. Peel the lemon and put the rind into a bowl. Add the chilli pepper, bay leaves and olive oil. Put the bowl into a pan of hot water and leave for 4hr. Rub the chicken joints with salt and pepper, brush them with the sauce and cook under a hot grill for 20min on each side, brushing the sauce over the chicken after 10min. Serve the chicken with the hot sauce, lemon slices and rice.

Chicken with Almond Sauce

4 chicken joints
3oz (75g, 6 tbsp) butter
2oz (50g, scant ⅓ cup) split almonds
1oz (25g, ¼ cup) flour
½pt (250ml, 1¼ cups) milk
1oz (25g, 1⅔ cups) ground almonds

Preparation time: about 30min   Cooking time: 35min

Sprinkle the chicken joints with salt and pepper. Melt 2oz (50g, 4 tbsp) of butter and fry the chicken joints for 20min, turning frequently. Remove the chicken and put on to a heated serving dish, keep hot. Put the split almonds into the butter and turning constantly, fry until the almonds are golden brown. Remove the almonds from the butter and keep hot. Make a white sauce (see page 13) with the remaining butter, milk and flour. Remove the sauce from the heat and stir in the ground almonds. Pour the almond sauce over the chicken and sprinkle the split almonds on top. Serve hot.

Coq au Vin*

2lb (1kg) chicken
1¼pt (625ml, 3¼ cups) red wine
1oz (25g, ¼ cup) flour
2 garlic cloves
4oz (100g, ½ cup) butter
12 shallots
8oz (250g) button mushrooms
2 tbsp (25ml, 2½ tbsp) brandy

Preparation time: about 40min   Cooking time: 1¾hr

Cut the chicken into neat joints and rub with salt and pepper. Melt half the butter in a large casserole and fry the shallots, mushrooms and chicken joints until golden brown. Add the garlic cloves, finely chopped. Pour the brandy over the chicken and set it alight. Add the red wine and simmer the chicken for 1½hr. Melt the remaining butter and remove the pan from the heat. Blend in the flour and then stir in a little of the juice from the casserole. Stir the thickened sauce into the casserole and continue cooking the chicken for a further 5min over a low heat. Serve hot with straw potatoes.

Spiced Chicken

2lb (1kg) chicken
4oz (100g) onions
3 tbsp (60ml, 4 tbsp) tomato purée
¾pt (375ml, 2 cups) stock
2oz (50g, 4 tbsp) butter
1 tbsp (10g, 1¼ tbsp) paprika pepper
¼pt (125ml, scant ¾ cup) sour cream

Preparation time: about 30min   Cooking time: 1¼hr

Peel and slice the onions. Cut the chicken into quarters. Melt the butter in a deep frying pan and fry the chicken, turning frequently, for 10min, then remove from the pan and fry the onions until soft. Stir in the tomato purée, paprika pepper, a pinch of cayenne pepper, salt and pepper to taste. Add the stock and bring to the boil. Put the chicken quarters into the pan and, basting frequently, simmer for 1hr. Stir in the sour cream and serve with plain rice.

Liver and Bacon Olives

6oz (150g) chicken livers
4oz (100g, 3 cups) white breadcrumbs
8oz (250g) streaky bacon
2oz (50g) onions
1 tbsp (10g, 1¼ tbsp) chopped parsley
1 egg
4oz (100g, ½ cup) dripping

Preparation time: about 35min   Cooking time: 30min

Peel and chop the onion. Cut the rinds from the bacon. Whisk the egg. Melt half the dripping and cook the chicken livers for 10min. Finely chop the chicken and mix with the breadcrumbs, onion, chopped parsley and egg. Add salt and pepper to taste. Put some of the liver mixture on each rasher of bacon, roll the bacon up and tie securely with white cotton. Melt the remaining dripping in a shallow casserole and put the bacon olives into the casserole. Cover and cook in a moderate oven, 350° F, 180° C, mark 4, for 20min. Serve hot.

Turkey Soufflé

12oz (350g) cooked turkey
1 tbsp (10g, 1¼ tbsp) chopped parsley
2oz (50g) onions
3 eggs
½pt (250ml, 1¼ cups) milk
2oz (50g, ½ cup) flour
2oz (50g, 4 tbsp) butter

Preparation time: about 40min   Cooking time: 45min

Pre-heat the oven to 375° F, 190° C, mark 5. Grease a 6in (15¼cm) soufflé dish. Peel and finely chop the onion. Mince the turkey. Separate the egg yolks from the egg whites. Make a white sauce (see page 13) with the butter, flour and milk. Stir the turkey, chopped parsley and onion into the sauce, adding salt and pepper to taste. Whisk the egg yolks lightly and stir into the turkey mixture. Whisk the egg whites until stiff and fold into the turkey. Pour the mixture into the prepared soufflé dish and cook in a moderately hot oven, 375° F, 190° C, mark 5, for 35min. Serve immediately.

Fillets of Turkey

8oz (250g) cooked turkey slices
4oz (100g) ham slices
4oz (100g) Mozzarella cheese
½pt (250ml, 1¼ cups) white wine
2oz (50g, ½ cup) pine nuts

Preparation time: about 20min   Cooking time: 20min

Put the turkey slices in the bottom of a greased casserole, then a layer of pine nuts, then a layer of ham and lastly top with a layer of Mozzarella cheese. Pour the wine over the top, cover and cook in a moderate oven, 350° F, 180° C, mark 4, for 20min.

Turkey Ham Bake*

12oz (350g) cooked turkey
8oz (250g) ham
2oz (50g) onions
2oz (50g, 4 tbsp) butter
2oz (50g, ¾ cup) dried breadcrumbs
4oz (100g) Cheddar cheese
2 tbsp (25ml, 2½ tbsp) sherry
1oz (25g, ¼ cup) flour
¼pt (125ml, scant ¾ cup) single cream
¼pt (125ml, scant ¾ cup) milk
4oz (100g) button mushrooms

Preparation time: about 35min   Cooking time: 35min

Peel and slice the onions. Clean and slice the mushrooms. Grate the cheese. Finely chop the turkey and ham. Melt half the butter and cook the onions until soft. Make a white sauce (see page 13) with the remaining butter, flour, milk, cream and salt and pepper to taste. Remove the sauce from the heat and stir in the sherry, turkey, ham, onions and mushrooms. Put the turkey mixture into a greased casserole, cover with the grated cheese and sprinkle the breadcrumbs round the top. Cook in a moderate oven, 350° F, 180° C, mark 4, for 20min. Serve hot.

VEGETABLES

Bean and Egg Layer

1½lb (750g) French beans
3oz (75g) Cheddar cheese
3 eggs
2oz (50g) onions
2oz (50g, 4 tbsp) butter
½pt (250ml, 1¼ cups) milk
1oz (25g, ¼ cup) flour
2oz (50g, ¾ cup) dried breadcrumbs

Preparation time: about 25min   Cooking time: 30min
Wash the beans in cold water, then cook in boiling, salted water
for 15min, or until tender. Drain and slice. Grate the cheese. Boil the
eggs for 10min and remove the shells, then slice. While the beans
are cooking, peel and finely chop the onions. Make a white sauce (see
page 13) with 1oz (25g) of butter, the milk and flour, stir in the onion
and keep hot. Put the beans and eggs in layers in a greased casserole
and pour the sauce over the top. Sprinkle on the cheese and breadcrumbs, dot with the remaining butter and cook in a moderate oven,
350° F, 180° C, mark 4, for 15min. Serve hot.

French Beans with Cheese

1½lb (750g) French beans
2oz (50g, 4 tbsp) butter
1oz (25g, ¼ cup) grated Parmesan cheese
1 garlic clove

Preparation time: about 15min   Cooking time: 20min
Pinch the ends and cook the beans in boiling salted water for 15min.
Peel and crush the garlic. Drain the beans, stir in the garlic and butter,
put into a casserole and cover with the cheese. Place under a hot grill
to melt the cheese. Serve hot.

Brussels Sprouts with Cheese Sauce

2lb (1kg) brussels sprouts
1oz (25g, 2 tbsp) butter
1oz (25g, ¼ cup) flour
½pt (250ml, 1¼ cups) milk
2oz (50g) Cheddar cheese

Preparation time: about 35min   Cooking time: 15min

Remove the outer leaves and stalks from the brussels sprouts and cut a cross in the bases. Cook the sprouts in boiling, salted water for 15min. Drain and put them into a dish to keep warm. While the sprouts are cooking, make a cheese sauce (see page 14) and pour over the cooked sprouts. Serve hot.

Brussels Sprouts with Chestnuts

2lb (1kg) brussels sprouts
12oz (375g) chestnuts
4oz (100g, ½ cup) butter

Preparation time: about 45min   Cooking time: 30min

Cut a cross in the skins of the chestnuts and put them in a saucepan of boiling, salted water for 20min. While the chestnuts are cooking, remove the outer leaves and the stalks from the brussels sprouts and cut a cross in the bases. Cook in a saucepan of boiling salted water for 15min. Drain the brussels sprouts and melt half the butter, then toss the sprouts in the butter and keep hot. Drain the chestnuts and remove the outer and inner skins. Melt the remaining butter and fry the chestnuts for 5min. Mix the brussels sprouts and chestnuts together. Serve hot.

Casseroled Beetroot

4 medium sized cooked beetroot
2oz (50g, 4 tbsp) butter
3 tbsp (50ml, 4 tbsp) red wine
¼pt (125ml, scant ¾ cup) sour cream

Preparation time: about 30min   Cooking time: 20min

Remove the skins and slice the beetroot finely, then put the slices into a shallow casserole. Melt the butter, mix with the red wine and pour over the beetroot. Sprinkle with salt, pepper and paprika pepper. Pour on the sour cream, cover with foil and cook in a moderate oven, 350° F, 180° C, mark 4, for 20min. Serve hot with the sauce.

Bavarian Cabbage

2lb (1kg) cabbage
4oz (100g) bacon
2oz (50g) onions
1oz (25g, ¼ cup) brown sugar
¼pt (125ml, scant ¾ cup) white wine
1 tsp (5g, 1¼ tsp) carraway seeds
2 tbsp (25ml, 2½ tsp) wine vinegar
½ gill (60ml, ⅓ cup) stock
1oz (25g, 2 tbsp) dripping

Preparation time: about 30min   Cooking time: 20min

Clean and shred the cabbage. Remove the rinds from the bacon and chop it. Peel and chop the onions. Melt the dripping and fry the bacon and onions over a low heat for 5min. Put the cabbage, bacon, onions and brown sugar in layers into a thick-bottomed saucepan. Sprinkle with the carraway seeds and salt and pepper. Add the wine vinegar and stock, cover tightly and cook over a low heat for 10min, stirring from time to time. Heat the wine and pour over the cabbage. Cook for a further 5min. Serve hot.

Red Cabbage

2lb (1kg) red cabbage
4oz (100g) onions
8oz (250g) apples
2oz (50g, 4 tbsp) butter
2oz (50g, $\frac{1}{2}$ cup) brown sugar
2 tbsp (25ml, 2$\frac{1}{2}$ tbsp) cider vinegar
$\frac{1}{4}$pt (125ml, scant $\frac{3}{4}$ cup) water

Preparation time: about 40min   Cooking time: 1$\frac{1}{4}$–1$\frac{1}{2}$hr
Finely shred the cabbage. Peel and finely slice the onion and apples.
Melt the butter in the bottom of a thick-bottomed saucepan. Put the
cabbage, onions, apples and brown sugar in layers in the saucepan and
sprinkle with salt and pepper. Add the cider vinegar and water, cover
tightly and cook over a very low heat for 1$\frac{1}{4}$–1$\frac{1}{2}$hr, stirring from time
to time to prevent sticking. Serve hot.

Baked Carrots

1½lb (750g) carrots
2oz (50g) onions
2oz (50g, 4 tbsp) butter
1oz (25g, 2 tbsp) sugar
½ gill (60ml, ⅓ cup) water
2oz (50g, ¾ cup) dried breadcrumbs

Preparation time: about 40min   Cooking time: 35min
Peel and roughly grate the carrots. Peel and chop the onions. Melt the butter and cook the onions over a low heat until soft. Mix the carrots, onions, sugar and water together, adding salt and pepper to taste. Grease a 2pt pie dish, put in the carrot mixture and sprinkle the breadcrumbs over the top. Bake in a moderate oven, 350° F, 180° C, mark 4, for 30min. Serve hot.

Celery Cooked in Tomato Sauce

2 celery heads
2oz (50g) onions
1 tbsp (10g, 1¼ tbsp) chopped parsley
2 tbsp (25ml, 2½ tbsp) oil for frying
Sauce
8oz (250g) soft tomatoes
3 tbsp (60ml, 4 tbsp) tomato purée
1 tbsp (15ml, 1¼ tbsp) Worcestershire sauce
1 tsp (5g, 1¼ tsp) dry mustard
2 tbsp (25ml, 2½ tbsp) wine vinegar
½oz (15g, 1 tbsp) butter
1 tsp (5g, 1¼ tsp) salt
1 tsp (5g, 1¼ tsp) paprika pepper

Preparation time: about 30min   Cooking time: 35min
Clean the celery and remove the green tops and coarse ends. Cut the celery into 3in (7·5cm) pieces and cook in boiling, salted water for 30min. While the celery is cooking, make the tomato sauce (see page 15). Peel and finely chop the onions then fry over a low heat for 5min. Stir the onions and chopped parsley into the tomato sauce. Drain the celery and keep warm in the saucepan. Pour the sauce over the celery and simmer for 5min. Serve hot.

French Fried Cauliflower

2lb (1kg) cauliflower
2 eggs
4oz (100g, 1½ cups) dried breadcrumbs

Preparation time: about 20min   Cooking time: 15min
Clean the cauliflower, removing the outer leaves, and break into
flowerets. Bring a saucepanful of salted water to the boil, drop in the
cauliflower and cook for 10min then drain. Whisk the eggs. Add salt
and pepper to the breadcrumbs. Dip the flowerets into the beaten egg,
then into the breadcrumbs. Heat enough oil for deep frying and fry
the cauliflower for 5min. Serve hot.

Chicory à la Crème

4 chicory heads
2oz (50g, 4 tbsp) butter
¼pt (125ml, scant ¾ cup) water
2 tbsp (25ml, 2½ tbsp) lemon juice
¼pt (125ml, scant ¾ cup) single cream

Preparation time: about 20min   Cooking time: 45min
Clean the chicory and remove any outer leaves, if discoloured. Melt
the butter in a saucepan. Add the chicory, water, lemon juice and salt
and pepper to taste. Cover tightly and cook over a low heat for
45min. Heat the cream and pour over. Take the chicory out of the
saucepan, put on to a serving dish and pour the sauce over the top.
Serve hot.

Corn Pudding

8oz (250g, 1 cup) tinned corn kernels
2 eggs
2oz (50g, 4 tbsp) butter
½pt (250ml, 1¼ cups) milk
1oz (25g, 2 tbsp) sugar

Preparation time: about 20min　　　　　　　　Cooking time: 45min

Drain the corn. Whisk the eggs lightly. Melt the butter and mix with corn kernels and sugar, adding salt and pepper to taste. Heat the milk and stir into the eggs. Put the corn mixture into a greased 2pt pie dish, pour on the milk and egg mixture. Put the dish in a roasting pan and half fill pan with water. Cook the corn pudding in a moderate oven, 350° F, 180° C, mark 4, for 40min. Top the water up, if necessary, during cooking. Serve hot.

Courgettes with Parmesan Cheese

1½lb (750g) courgettes
4oz (100g, ½ cup) butter
1oz (25g, ¼ cup) grated Parmesan cheese

Preparation time: about 15min　　　　　　　　Cooking time: 20min

Wash the courgettes in cold water, cut off the stalks and slice the courgettes into rounds. Melt the butter and simmer the slices in it for 20min. Sprinkle with salt and pepper. Serve the courgettes with the melted butter and sprinkle with the Parmesan cheese. Serve hot.

Ham and Courgettes Baked in Yogurt

6oz (150g) cooked ham
1lb (500g) courgettes
2oz (50g) cheese
2oz (50g) onions
¼pt (125ml, scant ¾ cup) plain yogurt
¼pt (125ml, scant ¾ cup) milk
1 egg
2oz (50g, 4 tbsp) butter

Preparation time: about 35min　　　　　　　　Cooking time: 30min

Grate the cheese. Peel and finely chop the onion. Cut the courgettes in half lengthways and carefully remove the centres. Finely dice the courgette centres and the ham. Mix the centres, ham and onion together. Melt the butter and cook this mixture for 10min, adding salt and pepper to taste. Put the ham mixture into the courgette halves and place them in a greased casserole.

Whisk the egg and mix together with the milk and yogurt. Pour round the stuffed courgettes. Sprinkle over the cheese and bake in a moderate oven, 350° F, 180° C, mark 4, for 20min. Serve hot.

Aubergine (Eggplant) Fritters

2 large aubergines
4oz (100g, 1 cup) flour
½pt (250ml, 1¼ cups) milk
1 egg

Preparation time: about 1hr   Cooking time: 15min

Cut off the stalks and slice aubergines in rounds, then put them on a plate and sprinkle with salt. Cover and leave for 30min. Make a thick batter (see page 12). Drain the aubergine and dry well with kitchen paper. Pour oil into a deep frying pan and heat. Coat the aubergine rounds with the batter and drop into the hot oil. Cook for 10–15min until crisp. Serve hot.

Egg and Vegetable Casserole

4 eggs
2 garlic cloves
2oz (50g) onions
8oz (250g) potatoes
2oz (50g) garlic sausage
2oz (50g) ham
6oz (150g) tomatoes
1 green pepper
4oz (100g, 1 cup) cooked peas

Preparation time: about 40min   Cooking time: 45min

Peel and crush the garlic cloves. Peel the potatoes and onions. Skin the tomatoes. Remove the centre core and seeds from the green pepper. Finely chop the potatoes, onions, tomatoes, pepper, garlic sausage and ham. Heat some oil and fry the potatoes for 15min, then remove and fry the onion, garlic sausage and ham over a low heat for 10min. Add the other vegetables, garlic and salt and pepper to taste. Fry over a low heat for another 10min. Put the fried ingredients into a shallow casserole. Whisk the eggs until frothy, pour over the vegetables and cook in a moderately hot oven, 375° F, 190° C, mark 5, for 10min. Serve hot.

Leeks with Cheese Sauce

2lb (1kg) leeks
1pt (500ml, 2½ cups) milk
2oz (50g, ½ cup) flour
2oz (50g, 4 tbsp) butter
4oz (100g) cheese

Preparation time: about 15min   Cooking time: 30min

Wash the leeks thoroughly and cut off the green top leaves and the roots. Cook over a low heat in boiling, salted water for 20–30min, testing with a knife for tenderness. When cooked, drain and put the leeks on to a hot serving plate. Keep hot. While the leeks are cooking, make a cheese sauce (see page 14) and pour over the leeks. Serve hot.

Braised Lettuce

2 small lettuce
4oz (100g) onions
3oz (75g, 6 tbsp) butter
1 tbsp (10g, 1¼ tbsp) chopped parsley
½oz (12g, scant ¼ cup) cornflour
½pt (250ml, 1¼ cups) stock
½ tsp (3g, 1¼ tsp) paprika pepper

Preparation time: about 30min   Cooking time: 50min

Clean the lettuces and remove any wilted outer leaves. Peel and slice the onion. Put the lettuces into a large saucepan of boiling salted water for 5min. Remove and plunge into cold water. Melt 2oz (50g, 4 tbsp) of the butter in a large casserole and put in the onions, paprika pepper, lettuces, stock and salt and pepper to taste. Cover tightly and simmer over a low heat for 30min. Drain the lettuce, keeping the stock and put into a large serving dish, keep hot. Melt the remaining butter in a saucepan, remove from the heat and stir in the cornflour and the stock. Replace the saucepan on the heat and stirring, cook until the sauce thickens. Stir in the chopped parsley and salt and pepper to taste. Pour the sauce over the lettuce. Serve hot.

Baked Mushrooms

1¼lb (750g) mushrooms
4oz (100g) onions
2oz (50g, 4 tbsp) butter
½pt (250ml, 1¼ cups) sour cream
½oz (12g, scant ¼ cup) cornflour
1 tbsp (10g, 1¼ tbsp) chopped parsley

Preparation time: about 30min   Cooking time: 25min

Wash and slice the mushrooms. Peel and slice the onions. Melt the butter and cook the onions over a low heat for 5min. Add the mushrooms and continue cooking for a further 10min. Put the mushrooms and onions into a casserole, adding salt and pepper to taste. Stir the cornflour and chopped parsley into the sour cream and pour over the mushrooms. Cover the casserole and cook in a slow oven, 325° F, 165° C, mark 3, for 10min. Serve hot.

Mushroom and Ham Casserole*

1lb (500g) mushrooms
4oz (100g) Cheddar cheese
8oz (250g) cooked ham
½pt (250ml, 1¼ cups) milk
1oz (25g, scant ⅓ cup) cornflour
2oz (50g, 4 tbsp) butter
1 tsp (5g, 1¼ tsp) ground paprika pepper

Preparation time: about 30min   Cooking time: 30min
Grate the cheese. Finely dice half the ham. Wash and slice the mushrooms. Melt half the butter and cook the mushrooms with the diced ham for 5min. Make a white sauce (see page 13) with the cornflour, remaining butter and the milk. Stir in the mushrooms, diced ham, half the cheese and ground paprika pepper. Slice the remaining ham and lay it flat in a shallow casserole, pour over the sauce and sprinkle on the rest of the cheese. Bake in a moderately hot oven, 375° F, 190° C, mark 5, for 10min. Serve hot.

Parsnips with Cheese Sauce

2lb (1kg) parsnips
½pt (250ml, 1¼ cups) milk
1oz (25g, ¼ cup) flour
2oz (50g, 4 tbsp) butter
2oz (50g) Cheddar cheese

Preparation time: about 30min   Cooking time: 47min
Clean and peel the parsnips, cut them into quarters lengthwise and remove the centre cores. Put the parsnips into a saucepanful of boiling water, add 1 tsp salt and cook for 45min. While the parsnips are cooking make the sauce. Grate the cheese. Using the milk, flour and 1oz (25g, 2 tbsp) of the butter, make a white sauce (see page 13). Drain the parsnips and put them into a shallow casserole. Cover with the white sauce and sprinkle with the grated cheese. Dot with butter and put under a hot grill for a couple of minutes to brown the top. Serve hot.

Stuffed Pancakes

Filling
2oz (50g) onions
1 green pepper
4oz (100g) mushrooms
6oz (150g) streaky bacon
6oz (150g) Cheddar cheese
2 tbsp (40ml, 2½ tbsp) tomato purée
2 tbsp (25ml, 2½ tbsp) oil
Batter
4oz (100g, 1 cup) flour
½pt (250ml, 1¼ cups) milk
1 egg
oil for frying

Preparation time: about 40min   Cooking time: 40min

Make a batter (see page 12). While the batter is standing, make the filling. Peel the onions. Remove the centre core and seeds from the green pepper. Clean the mushrooms and remove the rinds from the bacon. Grate the cheese. Finely chop the onions, pepper, mushrooms and bacon. Heat the oil and fry the onions and pepper over a low heat for 5min. Stir in the bacon, mushrooms and half the cheese. Add salt and pepper to taste and cook over a low heat for another 10min.

Heat some oil in a frying pan and pour in a little batter. Cook both sides of the pancake until browned, turn out and keep hot. Continue making pancakes until all the batter is used up. Put some filling in each pancake, roll up and place in a shallow casserole. Stir an equal amount of water into the tomato purée and pour over the pancakes. Sprinkle with the rest of the cheese and bake in a moderate oven, 350° F, 180° C, mark 4, for 15min. Serve hot.

Peas with Cheese

1lb (500g, 4 cups) frozen peas
2oz (50g) onions
2oz (50g, 4 tbsp) butter
4oz (100g) cheese
½ tsp (3g, ¾ tsp) dried basil
½ tsp (3g, ¾ tsp) dried marjoram
2 tbsp (25ml, 2½ tbsp) water
2oz (50g, ½ cup) olives

Preparation time: about 1hr   Cooking time: 10min

Defrost the peas. Grate the cheese. Peel and finely chop the onions. Put the peas, butter, basil, marjoram, onion and water into a saucepan, adding ½ tsp of salt and pepper. Cover the saucepan tightly and cook the peas over a low heat for 10min. Slice the olives and stir into the peas. Put the peas into a serving dish and cover with the grated cheese. Serve hot.

Pepperoni

2 green peppers
2 red peppers
6oz (150g) onions
1 garlic clove
3oz (75g, 6 tbsp) butter

Preparation time: about 20min   Cooking time: 20min

Remove the stalks, cores and seeds from the peppers and slice finely. Peel and slice the onions. Peel and crush the garlic. Melt the butter and cook the peppers, onions and garlic over a low heat for 20min. Add salt and pepper to taste. Serve hot.

Pizza*

1lb (500g) soft tomatoes
1 garlic clove
1 tbsp (15ml, 1¼ tbsp) olive oil
1 tsp (5g, 1¼ tsp) dried marjoram
4oz (100g) Mozzarella cheese
2oz (50g) tinned anchovy fillets
Shortcrust pastry
8oz (250g, 2 cups) plain flour
4oz (100g, ½ cup) fat

Preparation time: about 45min   Cooking time: 50min

Skin and finely chop the tomatoes. Peel and crush the garlic. Put the tomatoes, garlic, olive oil and marjoram into a saucepan and add salt and pepper to taste. Simmer over a low heat for 30min.

While the tomatoes are cooking, make the shortcrust pastry (see page 11). Roll the pastry into a rectangular shape to cover a baking sheet approximately 10in by 14½in (26cm by 37cm). Oil the baking sheet and lay on the pastry. Slice the Mozzarella cheese. Put the tomato pulp on the pastry and lay the slices of Mozzarella cheese on the tomatoes. Drain the anchovy fillets and arrange in a lattice pattern on the cheese. Bake in a moderately hot oven, 375° F, 190° C, mark 5, for 20min. Serve hot or cold.

French-style Potatoes

4oz (100g) Gruyère cheese
1½lb (750g) potatoes
6oz (150g) onions
3oz (75g, 6 tbsp) butter
¾pt (375ml, 2 cups) milk

Preparation time: about 30min   Cooking time: 1½hr

Grate the cheese. Peel and slice the potatoes and onions. Put half the butter in the bottom of a casserole, then arrange the potatoes, onions and cheese in layers in the casserole. Sprinkle each layer with salt and pepper. Dot with the remaining butter. Heat the milk and pour over the potatoes. Cook in a slow oven, 325° F, 165° C, mark 3, for 1½hr. Serve hot.

Potatoes Baked in Sour Cream

1½lb (750g) potatoes
4oz (100g) onions
4oz (100g) cheese
1oz (25g, 2 tbsp) butter
¼pt (125ml, scant ¾ cup) sour cream
1 egg
2oz (50g, ¾ cup) dried breadcrumbs

Preparation time: about 35min   Cooking time: 40min

Peel the potatoes and cook in boiling salted water for 20min. Peel and slice the onions. Grate the cheese. Melt the butter in a frying pan and cook the onions until soft. Drain the potatoes and slice them evenly. Arrange the potatoes, onions and cheese in layers in a casserole, sprinkle with salt and pepper. Whisk the egg and mix it into the sour cream, pour over the potatoes and sprinkle on the dried breadcrumbs. Cook in a moderate oven, 350° F, 180° C, mark 4, for 10min. Serve hot.

PASTA & RICE

To Cook Pasta*

8oz (250g) pasta
5¼pt (4l, 7pt) water
1 tsp (5g, 1¼ tsp) salt

Bring the water and salt to the boil, add the pasta and stir. Bring to
the boil again and boil rapidly for 2min. (If using a thick pasta, such
as macaroni, boil for 3min.) Remove the saucepan from the heat,
put a clean cloth under the lid and leave for the exact cooking time
mentioned on the side of the packet. The pasta should then be 'al
dente', firm to the bite and not soft, but with a certain elasticity.
Drain and serve with butter and grated Parmesan cheese or a sauce.

Buried Ham in Macaroni

8oz (250g) macaroni
5¼pt (4l, 7pt) water
8oz (250g) ham
2 eggs
4oz (100g) Cheddar cheese
¼pt (125ml, scant ¾ cup) sour cream

Preparation time: about 20min   Cooking time: 22min
Break the macaroni into small pieces and cook (see above). Grate
the cheese. Whisk the eggs. Finely chop the ham. Drain the macaroni,
stir in the ham and put into a greased casserole. Mix together the eggs
and sour cream, add salt and pepper and pour over the ham and
macaroni. Sprinkle the cheese over the ham and macaroni and cook in
a moderate oven, 350° F, 180° C, mark 4, for 10min. Serve hot.

Buttered Shell Noodles

8oz (250g) shell noodles
5¼pt (4l, 7pt) water
8oz (250g) mushrooms
2oz (50g) onions
1 tbsp (10g, 1¼ tbsp) chopped parsley
4oz (100g, ½ cup) butter

96

Preparation time: about 30min   Cooking time: 25min

Cook the shell noodles (see page 96). Peel and finely chop the onion. Clean and slice the mushrooms. Melt the butter in a large frying pan and cook the onions and mushrooms over a low heat for 5min. When the noodles are cooked, drain them and put into the frying pan. Add the chopped parsley and salt and pepper to taste, then stir gently over a low heat for 5min. Serve hot.

Lasagne al Forno (Baked Wide Noodles)*

8oz (250g) lasagne
5¼pt (4l, 7pt) water
4oz (100g, 1 cup) grated Parmesan cheese
White sauce
1pt (500ml, 2½ cups) milk
2oz (50g, ½ cup) flour
2oz (50g, 4 tbsp) butter
Sauce Bolognese
8oz (250g, 1 cup) minced beef
4oz (100g) onions
1 garlic clove
2 tbsp (40ml, 2½ tbsp) tomato purée
8oz (250g) soft tomatoes
¼pt (125ml, scant ¾ cup) stock
½ gill (60ml, ⅓ cup) olive oil
1 tsp (5g, 1¼ tsp) sugar

Preparation time: about 45min   Cooking time: 1hr and 5min

Make a sauce Bolognese (see page 15). While it is cooking, cook the lasagne (see page 96) and make a white sauce (see page 13). When the pasta is cooked take the sheets from the saucepan and pat them dry on a clean tea-towel. Grease a square casserole, put a layer of pasta on the bottom, then spread with sauce Bolognese, then pasta, then white sauce. Continue in this way until all the ingredients have been used up, the top layer being of white sauce. Sprinkle on the Parmesan cheese and bake in a moderate oven, 350° F, 180° C, mark 4, for 30min. Serve hot.

Canneloni*

8 canneloni
5¼pt (4l, 7pt) water
8oz (250g) mushrooms
3oz (75g, 6 tbsp) butter
2oz (50g, ½ cup) flour
1pt (500ml, 2½ cups) milk
3oz (75g, scant ¾ cup) grated Parmesan cheese

Preparation time: about 25min   Cooking time: 45min

Cook the canneloni tubes (see page 96). Clean the mushrooms and finely slice. Melt 1oz (25g, 2 tbsp) of butter and cook the mushrooms over a low heat for 5min. Make a white sauce (see page 13) with the remaining butter, flour and milk. Stir the mushrooms into half the sauce, adding salt and pepper to taste. Drain the canneloni tubes and fill them with the sauce. Put the canneloni into a greased shallow casserole, pour over the remaining sauce and sprinkle on the Parmesan cheese and cook in a low oven, 325° F, 165° C, mark 3, for 30min.

Pepper Noodle Bake

6oz (150g) noodles
5¼pt (4l, 7pt) water
2 eggs
4oz (100g) Cheddar cheese
2 tbsp (25ml, 2½ tbsp) milk
1 green pepper

Preparation time: about 30min   Cooking time: 50min

Cook the noodles (see page 96). Separate the egg yolks from the whites. Whisk the yolks and stiffly beat the whites. Grate the cheese. Remove the core and seeds from the pepper and finely chop it. Drain the noodles and mix together with the egg yolks, cheese, green pepper and milk, adding salt and pepper to taste. Fold in the egg whites. Grease a 6in cake tin and pour in the noodle mixture. Put this tin into a roasting tin, with enough water to come half-way up the side of the cake tin. Steam in a moderate oven, 350° F, 180° C, mark 4, for 40min. Turn out and serve hot.

Casseroled Shrimps with Butterfly Noodles*

8oz (250g) butterfly noodles
5¼pt (4l, 7pt) water
8oz (250g) mushrooms
6oz (150g, 1½ cups) peas
4oz (100g) Cheddar cheese
1pt (350g, ¾lb) shelled shrimps
White sauce
½pt (250ml, 1¼ cups) milk
1oz (25g, ¼ cup) flour
1oz (25g, 2 tbsp) butter

Preparation time: about 30min   Cooking time: 40min

Clean the mushrooms and slice finely. Cook the butterfly noodles (see page 96). Cook the peas in boiling water for 15min. Grate the cheese. Make a white sauce (see page 13), and when cooked stir in half the grated cheese. Drain the butterfly noodles and put them with the shrimps, mushrooms and peas in layers in a casserole. Pour over the sauce. Sprinkle with the remaining cheese and bake in a moderate oven, 350° F, 180° C, mark 4, for 25min. Serve hot.

Spaghetti Cheese Bake

8oz (250g) spaghetti
5¼pt (4l, 7pt) water
1lb 12oz (793g, 3½ cups) tinned tomatoes
8oz (250g) mushrooms
4oz (100g) onions
8oz (250g) ham
4oz (100g) Cheddar cheese
3oz (75g, 6 tbsp) butter
1 tsp (5g, 1¼ tsp) oregano

Preparation time: about 30min   Cooking time: 30min

Peel and slice the onions. Clean and slice the mushrooms and finely chop the ham. Grate the cheese. Cook the spaghetti (see page 96). While it is cooking, melt half the butter and cook the onions, mushrooms and ham over a low heat for 5min. Melt the rest of the butter in a large casserole and add the drained spaghetti. Stir well with the butter. Put the onions, mushrooms and ham on top of the spaghetti and add salt and pepper to taste. Pour on the contents of the tin of tomatoes, sprinkle the oregano and grated cheese over the top and bake in a moderate oven, 350° F, 180° C, mark 4, for 20min. Serve hot.

Tagliatelle Verde with Almonds

8oz (250g) tagliatelle verde
5¼pt (4l, 7pt) water
3oz (75g, scant ¾ cup) split almonds
3oz (75g, 6 tbsp) butter

Preparation time: about 10min   Cooking time: 15min

Cook the tagliatelle (see page 96). Melt the butter and cook the almonds for about 2min, until lightly browned. When cooked, drain the tagliatelle and toss in the butter and almonds. Stir gently and serve hot with grated Parmesan cheese.

Tomato Macaroni with Frankfurters

8oz (250g) macaroni
5¼pt (4l, 7pt) water
1lb (500g) frankfurters
4oz (100g) Cheddar cheese
2 tbsp (40ml, 2½ tbsp) tomato purée
2oz (50g, 4 tbsp) butter
1 tsp (5g, 1¼ tsp) oregano

Preparation time: about 30min   Cooking time: 22min

Break the macaroni into small pieces and cook (see page 96). While this is cooking, plunge the frankfurters in boiling water and cook for 5min. Grate the cheese. Drain the macaroni and frankfurters. Melt the butter and toss in the macaroni then put into a casserole. Arrange the frankfurters on top of the macaroni, mix the tomato purée with an equal amount of water, stir in the oregano, add salt and pepper and pour over the frankfurters and macaroni. Sprinkle on the cheddar cheese and cook in a moderate oven, 350° F, 180° C, mark 4, for 10min. Serve hot.

Tuna Tortiglioni Bake*

8oz (250g) tortiglioni
5¼pt (4l, 7pt) water
12oz (350g, 1¾ cups) tinned tuna fish
4oz (100g) onions
1 tbsp (10g, 1¼ tbsp) chopped parsley
¼pt (125ml, scant ¾ cup) single cream
1 tbsp (20ml, 1¼ tbsp) tomato purée
2 tbsp (25ml, 2½ tbsp) olive oil
White sauce
½pt (250ml, 1¼ cups) milk
1oz (25g, ¼ cup) flour
1oz (25g, 2 tbsp) butter

Preparation time: about 30min   Cooking time: 30min

Cook the tortiglioni (see page 96). Make a white sauce (see page 13). Drain the tortiglioni and keep warm. Peel and finely chop the onions, then heat the oil and cook them until soft. Stir in the tortiglioni, tuna fish, chopped parsley, and salt and pepper to taste. Put the tortiglioni mixture into a casserole and keep hot. Stir the tomato purée and cream into the white sauce and pour over the tortiglioni. Bake in a moderate oven, 350° F, 180° C, mark 4, for 10min. Serve hot.

To Cook Rice*

8oz (250g, 1¼ cups) long grain rice
1pt (500ml, 2½ cups) water
1 tsp (5g, 1¼ tsp) salt

Preparation time: about 5min   Cooking time: 20min

Bring the water to the boil in a large saucepan, add the salt and sprinkle in the rice. Bring the water to the boil again, stir the rice and lower the heat to simmering point. Cover the saucepan with a tight-fitting lid and leave the rice to simmer for 20min, or until the water has been absorbed. Remove from the heat and serve.

Rice, Bacon and Corn Bake*

6oz (150g, ⅞ cup) long grain rice
¾pt (375ml, 2 cups) water
8oz (250g) soft tomatoes
4oz (100g, ½ cup) butter
8oz (250g) streaky bacon
11½oz (376g, 1¾ cups) creamed corn

Preparation time: about 30min   Cooking time: 45min

Skin and slice the tomatoes. Cook the rice (see above). Melt half the butter and fry the bacon for 5min. Remove the bacon and toss the rice in the butter. Put the rice in the bottom of a greased casserole, place the creamed corn on top of the rice, then the bacon and lastly the sliced tomatoes. Add salt and pepper and dot with the remaining butter. Cook in a moderate oven, 350° F, 180° C, mark 4, for 20min. Serve hot.

Baked Rice Savoury Squares

6oz (150g, ⅞ cup) long grain rice
¾pt (375ml, 2 cups) water
2oz (50g) onions
8oz (250g) tomatoes
4oz (100g) Cheddar cheese
8oz (250g, 1 cup) minced meat
¼pt (125ml, scant ¾ cup) stock
2 eggs
2 tbsp (25ml, 2½ tbsp) oil

Preparation time: about 25min   Cooking time: 50min
Peel and finely chop the onions. Skin and finely chop the tomatoes.
Grate the cheese. Cook the rice (see page 102). Heat the oil and cook
the onions over a low heat for 5min, stir in the meat and when browned,
add the tomatoes, stock and salt and pepper to taste. Simmer for 10min.
Mix together the rice and meat mixture, whisk the eggs and fold
into the rice. Grease a square baking tin and put in the rice, press down
evenly and bake in a moderately hot oven, 375° F, 190° C, mark 5,
for 30min, turn out and serve hot.

Curried Rice*

8oz (250g, 1¼ cups) long grain rice
1pt (500ml, 2½ cups) water
4oz (100g) onions
1 tbsp (10g, 1¼ tbsp) curry powder
3oz (75g, 6 tbsp) butter

Preparation time: about 15min   Cooking time: 27min
Peel and finely chop the onions. Melt half the butter and cook the
onions over a low heat for 5min, stir in the curry powder, add salt
and pepper to taste and cook for a further minute. Add the rice and
water and simmer for 20min, stirring occasionally, until all the water
has been absorbed. Melt the rest of the butter and stir into the rice.
Serve hot or cold.

Chinese Rice Balls

8oz (250g, 1¼ cups) long grain rice
1pt (500ml, 2½ cups) chicken stock
2oz (50g, ½ cup) grated Parmesan cheese
4oz (100g) mushrooms
1 garlic clove
2oz (50g) onions
4oz (100g, 1½ cups) dried breadcrumbs
2oz (50g) Mozzarella cheese
3 eggs

Preparation time: about 45min   Cooking time: 35min

Peel and finely chop the onions. Clean and finely chop the mushrooms. Peel and crush the garlic. Finely chop the Mozzarella cheese. Cook the rice with the chicken stock (see page 102). Whisk 2 eggs and when the rice has absorbed all the stock, stir the beaten eggs and Parmesan

cheese into the rice, with salt and pepper to taste. Leave to get cold.

Heat some oil and cook the mushrooms, onions and garlic for 5min. Roll the rice into twelve balls and make a well in the centre of each ball. Mix together the onion, mushroom and Mozzarella cheese and put some of the mixture into the centres of each rice ball. Fold over the rice and seal by rolling gently in the palms of the hands. Whisk the remaining egg and dip in each rice ball, then roll in the breadcrumbs. Heat some oil and fry the rice balls until golden brown, for about 10min. Serve hot.

Nasi Goreng (Fried Rice)

8oz (250g, 1¼ cups) long grain rice
1pt (500ml, 2½ cups) water
4oz (100g) smoked pork ring
4oz (100g) bacon
½pt (175g, 6oz) peeled shrimps
2oz (50g) onions
1 garlic clove
2 tbsp (25ml, 2½ tbsp) oil
2 eggs
1oz (25g, 2 tbsp) butter
½ tsp (3g, ¾ tsp) chilli pepper
2 tbsp (25ml, 2½ tbsp) soya sauce
1 tsp (5g, 1¼ tsp) brown sugar
4oz (100g) cucumber

Preparation time: about 30min   Cooking time: 35min

Remove the rind from the bacon. Peel the onion. Finely chop the smoked pork, bacon, onion and garlic clove. Cook the rice (see page 102) and while it is cooking, mix together the chilli pepper, soya sauce and brown sugar. Heat the oil and cook the onion and garlic over a low heat for 5min, add the smoked pork, bacon, shrimps and soya sauce and cook over a low heat for 10min. Stir in the rice and continue cooking for 5min. Turn out on to a hot dish and keep hot.

Slice the cucumber finely. Whisk the eggs, adding salt and pepper to taste. Heat the butter in a frying pan and make four thin omelettes. Slice the omelettes into strips and garnish the rice with the cucumber and omelette strips.

Rice and Olive Stuffing

12oz (350g, 1¾ cups) long grain rice
4oz (100g, ½ cup) butter
8oz (250g) mushrooms
4oz (100g) celery
2oz (50g) onions
4oz (100g) ham
½ tsp (3g, ¾ tsp) marjoram
½ tsp (3g, ¾ tsp) sage
½ tsp (3g, ¾ tsp) thyme
1½pt (750ml, 3¼ cups) water
4oz (100g, 1 cup) black olives

Preparation time: about 25min   Cooking time: 25min

Clean the mushrooms and celery. Peel the onions. Finely chop the mushrooms, celery, ham and onions. Melt the butter in a large frying pan and add the rice, mushrooms, celery, ham, onion, marjoram, sage and thyme with salt and pepper to taste. Cook over a low heat for 5min, pour on the water and simmer gently, stirring occasionally for 20min, or until all the water has been absorbed. While the rice is cooking, stone and finely chop the olives. Add them to the rice and mix well. Leave to cool.

This amount of stuffing will stuff a 9–10lb (4½–5kg) turkey.

Salad Rice*

6oz (150g, ⅞ cup) long grain rice
¾pt (375ml, 2 cups) water
4oz (100g) young carrots
2oz (50g) onions
1 green pepper
2oz (50g, ½ cup) currants

Preparation time: about 50min   Cooking time: 20min

Cook the rice (see page 102). Leave to get cold. Peel and finely dice the carrots and onions. Remove the centre core and seeds from the pepper and finely dice. Mix together the carrots, pepper, onions, currants and rice, with salt and pepper to taste. Pour French dressing (see page 16) over the rice and stir gently with a fork.

Shrimp Risotto*

8oz (250g, 1¼ cups) long grain rice
1pt (500ml, 2½ cups) water
1pt (350g, ¾lb) peeled shrimps
4oz (100g) onions
1 green pepper
4oz (100g) mushrooms
1oz (25g, ¼ cup) grated Parmesan cheese
4 tbsp (65ml, ⅓ cup) olive oil

Preparation time: about 40min   Cooking time: 35min

Peel and finely chop the onion. Remove the centre core and seeds from the green pepper. Clean the mushrooms. Finely chop the green pepper and mushrooms. Heat half the oil in a large frying pan, add the rice, onion, green pepper and mushrooms and cook over a low heat for 10min, stirring all the time. Add the water and salt and pepper to taste. Cover and simmer for 20min until all the liquid has been absorbed. Heat the remaining oil and toss the rice and shrimps in it, then cook over a low heat for a further 5min. Serve hot with grated Parmesan cheese, or cold.

Stuffed Tomatoes

4oz (100g, ½ cup) long grain rice
½ pt (250ml, 1¼ cups) water
8 firm tomatoes
4oz (100g) onions
1oz (25g, ¼ cup) pine nuts
1 tbsp (10g, 1¼ tbsp) chopped parsley
1 tbsp (10g, 1¼ tbsp) chopped mint
1oz (25g, ⅓ cup) dried breadcrumbs
1oz (25g, ¼ cup) currants
2 tbsp (25ml, 2½ tbsp) olive oil

Preparation time: about 30min   Cooking time: 50min

Cook the rice (see page 102). While the rice is cooking, peel and finely chop the onions. Neatly cut off the tops of the tomatoes, carefully scoop out the pulp and finely chop. Heat half the oil and cook the onions over a low heat for 5min. Add the tomato pulp, mint, parsley, pine nuts and currants and cook for a further 2min, adding salt and pepper to taste.

When the rice is cooked, stir in the tomato mixture and stuff the tomatoes with the rice filling. Brush the tomatoes with the remaining olive oil and sprinkle with the breadcrumbs. Grease a baking sheet and place the tomatoes on it. Bake in a moderate oven, 350° F, 180° C, mark 4, for 30min. Serve hot or cold.

PUDDINGS

Apple and Date Scallop*

1lb (500g) cooking apples
4 tbsp (65ml, ⅓ cup) golden syrup
2oz (50g, ¼ cup) castor sugar
2oz (50g, ½ cup) flour
4oz (100g, ½ cup) stoned dates
2oz (50g, 1½ cups) white breadcrumbs
2oz (50g, 4 tbsp) butter
1 tsp (5g, 1¼ tsp) ground cinnamon

Preparation time: about 30min   Cooking time: 40min

Grease a 2pt pie dish. Finely chop the dates. Beat the butter and sugar until light and creamy, and stir in the flour, cinnamon and breadcrumbs. Peel, core and slice the apples. Put the apples, dates and golden syrup in the pie dish, cover with the topping and some greaseproof paper. Cook in a moderate oven, 350° F, 180° C, mark 4, for 30min, then remove the greaseproof paper and cook for a further 10min. Serve hot.

Apple Fool*

1½lb (750g) cooking apples
¼pt (125ml, scant ¾ cup) water
4oz (100g, ½ cup) sugar
½pt (250ml, 1¼ cups) double cream

Preparation time: about 20min   Cooking time: 10min

Peel, core and slice the apples. Put the apples, water and sugar into a saucepan and cook until soft. Rub through a fine nylon sieve and leave to get cold. Whip the cream until stiff and fold into the apple purée. Serve chilled in a glass bowl with sponge fingers.

Apple Fritters

1lb (500g) apples
4oz (100g, 1 cup) flour
1 egg
¼pt (125ml, scant ¾ cup) milk
2oz (50g, ¼ cup) sugar

Preparation time: about 30min   Cooking time: 10min

Make a batter (see page 12). Peel, core and slice the apples. Pierce a slice of apple with a skewer and dip into the batter. Heat some oil and drop the coated apple into the oil and cook until golden brown. Keep hot. Continue until all the apple slices are coated and cooked, then sprinkle with sugar and serve hot.

Apricot Cream*

6oz (150g, ¾ full cup) dried apricots
1 lemon
2oz (50g, ¼ cup) castor sugar
¼pt (125ml, scant ¾ cup) double cream
1oz (25g, ¼ cup) chopped walnuts

Preparation time: about 45min   Cooking time: 1hr
Chilling time: 2hr

Squeeze out the lemon juice. Put the apricots into a saucepan, cover with water and cook over a low heat until soft—about 1hr. Check the water during the cooking and add more, if necessary, to prevent burning. When the apricots are cooked, stir in the sugar and lemon juice, stirring thoroughly until the sugar has dissolved. Rub the apricots and juice through a nylon sieve or put into a liquidiser, to make into a purée, then allow to cool. Beat the cream until thick and fold into the purée. Pour the apricot cream into a glass bowl, and leave to chill in a refrigerator or cold larder for 2hr. Sprinkle with the chopped walnuts and serve with sponge fingers.

Banana Rolls

8oz (250g, 2 cups) flour
4oz (100g, ½ cup) fat
4 bananas
2oz (50g, ½ cup) Demerara sugar
½ tsp (3g, ¾tsp) ground nutmeg
1oz (25g, 1¼ tbsp) castor sugar
4 tbsp (65ml, ⅓ cup) jam
1 tbsp (15ml, 1¼ tbsp) milk

Preparation time: about 40min   Cooking time: 40min
Using the flour, fat and a little cold water make some shortcrust
pastry (see page 11). Roll out the dough into a rectangle and cut into
eight 3in (7·5cm) squares. Peel the bananas and cut each into half. Put
a banana half on each square of pastry, sprinkling with demerara sugar,
ground nutmeg and some jam. Fold the pastry over and pinch the
edges together, make four slits in the top and brush with milk. Sprinkle
with castor sugar and bake in a hot oven, 425° F, 220° C, mark 7, for
10min, then lower the heat to 350° F, 180° C, mark 4 and bake for
a further 30min. Serve hot or cold.

Blackberry Popovers

4oz (100g) blackberries
4oz (100g, 1 cup) self-raising flour
½pt (250ml, 1¼ cups) milk
1 egg
2oz (50g, ¼ cup) castor sugar
1oz (25g, 2 tbsp) butter

Preparation time: about 45min   Cooking time: 30min
Clean and rinse the blackberries in cold water, then dry on kitchen
paper. Heat the oven to 450° F, 230° C, mark 8. Make a batter with
the flour, milk and egg (see page 12). Melt a little butter in four
popover tins. Pour a quarter of the batter into each mould, then
the blackberries. Top with sugar and cook in the preheated oven for
30min. Turn out and sprinkle with castor sugar. Serve hot with
cream.

Brown Betty*

1½lb (750g) cooking apples
4oz (100g, 1 cup) brown sugar
2oz (50g, 4 tbsp) butter
6oz (150g, 3½ cups) white breadcrumbs
½ tsp (3g, ¾ tsp) cinnamon
1 lemon
¼pt (125ml, scant ¾ cup) water

Preparation time: about 35min   Cooking time: 1hr

Grate the lemon rind and squeeze out the juice. Melt the butter and mix with the breadcrumbs. Peel, core and slice the apples. Grease a 2pt pie dish and put the apples and breadcrumbs in alternate layers, sprinkling each layer with lemon rind, sugar and cinnamon. Mix together the lemon juice and water and pour over the apple and breadcrumbs. Bake in a moderate oven, 350° F, 180° C, mark 4, for 1hr. Serve hot.

Cinnamon Banana Fingers

4oz (100g) white bread slices
4 bananas
¼pt (125ml, scant ¾ cup) single cream
2oz (50g, ½ cup) Demerara sugar
2 tsp (12g, 2½ tsp) ground cinnamon
4oz (100g, ½ cup) butter

Preparation time: about 45min   Cooking time: 25min

Mix the cinnamon and sugar together. Remove the crusts from the bread and cut the slices in half. Lay the bread in a shallow dish and pour over the cream; leave for 15min. Remove the bread from the cream and coat with the cinnamon and sugar. Peel the bananas and cut in half lengthways. Melt half the butter and fry the bananas until soft—about 15min. Remove the bananas from the pan and keep hot. Melt the remaining butter and fry the sugar-coated bread until crisp, turning once—about 5–10min. Remove the bread from the pan and put a slice of banana on each piece of bread. Serve hot with cream or ice-cream.

Cheese Cake*

8oz (250g, 2 cups) flour
4oz (100g, ½ cup) fat
1lb (500g, 2 cups) cream cheese
2 eggs
3oz (75g, ⅓ cup) castor sugar
1 lemon
1oz (25g, scant ¼ cup) cornflour
2oz (50g, ½ cup) currants

Preparation time: about 40min   Cooking time: 45min

Grate the rind from the lemon and squeeze out the juice. Make the
shortcrust pastry (see page 11), roll out the dough and line a deep 8in
(21·5cm) flan tin. Separate the egg yolks from the egg whites. Beat
the yolks and castor sugar together until light and creamy. Fold in the
cream cheese, cornflour, currants, grated lemon rind and lemon juice;
stir well. Whisk the egg whites until stiff and fold into the cream cheese
mixture. Pour the mixture into the prepared pastry case and bake in
a moderate oven, 350° F, 180° C, mark 4, for 45min. Serve hot or
cold.

Clafouti

4oz (100g, 1 cup) plain flour
½pt (250ml, 1¼ cups) milk
2 eggs
2oz (50g, ¼ cup) sugar
12oz (350g) black cherries

Preparation time: about 45min   Cooking time: 30min

Heat the oven to 450° F, 230° C, mark 8. Stone the cherries. Make a
batter with the flour, milk and eggs (see page 12) and when smooth
stir in the sugar. Grease a shallow baking tin and put the cherries on
the bottom of the tin. Pour over the batter and bake in the preheated
oven for 30min. Leave to get cold and then turn the clafouti out of
the tin. Sprinkle with castor sugar.

  You can also make clafouti using any fruit such as apricots or
peaches.

Granny's Bread Pudding

8oz (250g) stale white bread
2oz (50g, ½ cup) sultanas
1oz (25g, ¼ cup) currants
2oz (50g, ⅓ cup) raisins
1oz (25g, ⅓ cup) mixed peel
4oz (100g, 1 cup) brown sugar
3oz (75g, 6 tbsp) butter
2 eggs
¼pt (125ml, scant ¾ cup) milk

Preparation time: about 2½hr   Cooking time: 1½hr

Soak the bread in cold water for 2hr, then squeeze out as much of the water as possible and beat the bread well with a fork. Whisk the eggs and melt the butter. Add the sultanas, currants, raisins, mixed peel and brown sugar, melted butter, eggs and milk to the bread; stir well. Line and grease a 6in (15·5cm) loaf tin and pour in the mixture. Bake in a moderate oven, 325° F, 165° C, mark 3, for 1½hr. Turn out and serve hot or cold in slices.

Danish Apple Pudding*

1lb (500g) cooking apples
6oz (150g, 2¼ cups) dried dark rye breadcrumbs
2oz (50g, 4 tbsp) butter
2oz (50g, ¼ cup) sugar
2oz (50g) cooking chocolate
4 tbsp (65ml, ⅓ cup) water
¼pt (125ml, scant ¾ cup) double cream
2 tbsp (25ml, 2½ tbsp) redcurrant jelly

Preparation time: about 30min   Cooking time: 10min

Grate the chocolate. Peel, core and slice the apples then put them and the water into a saucepan and cook until soft. Rub through a fine nylon sieve and leave to cool. While the apples are cooking, melt the butter and cook over a low heat with the breadcrumbs and sugar until crisp, stir in the chocolate and leave to cool. Put a layer of the breadcrumbs in a glass bowl, then a layer of apple purée. Continue in layers until all the ingredients are finished, making the last layer one of breadcrumbs. Whip the cream and pour over the breadcrumbs, then dot with the redcurrant jelly. Serve cold.

College Pudding

4oz (100g, 1 cup) shredded suet
4oz (100g, 3 cups) white breadcrumbs
2oz (50g, ½ cup) currants
2oz (50g, ½ cup) sultanas
1oz (25g, ⅓ cup) candied peel
1 egg
1 tsp (5g, 1¼ tsp) baking powder
4oz (100g, 1 cup) plain flour
2 tbsp (25ml, 2½ tbsp) golden syrup
½ gill (60ml, ⅓ cup) milk
pinch ground nutmeg

Preparation time: about 35min   Cooking time: 45min

Rub the flour, baking powder and nutmeg through a sieve. Mix together in a large mixing bowl, adding the suet, breadcrumbs, currants, sultanas and candied peel. Whisk the egg and mix with the golden syrup. Stir in all the other ingredients, adding enough milk to make a dropping consistency. Grease a 2pt pudding basin and pour the mixture into this, then cover with greaseproof paper. Put the pudding basin into a large saucepan, pour hot water around the basin and steam the pudding for 45min, topping up the hot water if necessary. Turn the pudding out and serve with a hot jam sauce.

Individual Chocolate Mousses*

2 eggs
4oz (100g) cooking chocolate
2 tbsp (25ml, 2½ tbsp) black coffee
1 tbsp (15ml, 1¼ tbsp) brandy
½oz (12g, 1 tbsp) butter

Preparation time: about 20min   Cooking time: 10min
Chilling time: 3hr

Separate the egg yolks from the egg whites. Whisk the yolks until light and frothy. Break the cooking chocolate into the top half of a double saucepan, add the coffee, brandy and butter and cook over hot water until the chocolate melts. Remove the pan from the heat and stir in the egg yolks. Whisk the egg whites until stiff and fold the chocolate mixture into the egg whites. Pour the chocolate mixture into four small glass or mousse pots. Leave to chill about 3hr. Serve with whipped cream.

Lemon Cream

2 lemons
3oz (75g, 6 tbsp) sugar
2 egg yolks
1oz (25g, scant ¼ cup) cornflour
½pt (250ml, 1¼ cups) water
½oz (12g, 1 tbsp) butter
14½oz (410g, 1¾ cups) tin evaporated milk

Preparation time: overnight and about 40min   Cooking time: 5min

Chill the evaporated milk overnight. Next day, grate the lemons

117

and squeeze out the juice. Mix the cornflour with a little of the water to make a smooth mixture and stir in the lemon juice. Heat the rest of the water and pour it on to the cornflour. Stir well and pour the mixture into the top half of a double saucepan and, stirring all the time, cook over hot water for 5min. Stir in the butter, lemon rind and sugar, and leave to cool for 5min. Beat in each egg yolk and leave to go cold, beating occasionally to prevent a skin forming. Beat the evaporated milk until stiff and fold into the lemon cream. Leave to set and decorate with glacé cherries if desired.

Lemon Sponge

2 lemons
3 eggs
½oz (12g, 1 envelope) gelatine
3 tbsp (50ml, 4 tbsp) warm water
¼pt (125ml, scant ¾ cup) double cream
3oz (75g, ⅓ cup) castor sugar

Preparation time: about 40min   Cooking time: 10min

Grate the lemon rinds and squeeze out the juice. Separate the egg yolks from the whites. Beat the yolks with the sugar until thick and creamy white, then put into the top half of a double saucepan. Add the lemon rind and juice. Stirring, cook over hot water until the mixture thickens. Dissolve the gelatine in the warm water and stir into the lemon mixture. Leave to cool. Whip the cream until thick and beat the egg whites until stiff. Fold the cream into the lemon mixture, then fold in the egg whites. Pour the mixture into a glass bowl and put into the refrigerator to chill. Serve with sponge fingers.

Meringue Pudding

3 egg whites
3oz (75g, ⅓ cup) castor sugar
2oz (50g, ½ cup) almond nibs
½ tsp (3g, ¾ tsp) almond essence
4 tbsp (65ml, ⅓ cup) jam

Preparation time: about 20min   Cooking time: 30min
Grease a 6in (15·5cm) soufflé dish. Whisk the egg whites until stiff and slowly add the sugar while continuing to whisk. Fold in the almond nibs. Put the jam in the bottom of the soufflé dish and pile in the meringue. Place the dish into a roasting tin and pour water into the roasting tin so that it comes half-way up the side of the soufflé dish. Cook in a slow oven, 275° F, 135° C, mark 1, for 30min. Serve the pudding hot or cold with cream.

Orange Meringue Rice Pudding

4oz (100g, ½ cup) Carolina rice
1pt (500ml, 2½ cups) milk
4oz (100g, ½ cup) castor sugar
2 eggs
1 orange
3oz (75g, ¼ cup) jam

Preparation time: about 30min   Cooking time: 1hr and 5min
Put the rice, milk and half the sugar into the top half of a double saucepan and heat to near boiling point over hot water, then simmer gently for 50min. Grate the orange rind, squeeze out the juice, then stir the rind and juice into the rice. Separate the egg yolks from the egg whites. Whisk the yolks and stir into the rice. Grease a 2pt pie dish and put in the jam, then pour on the orange-flavoured rice. Beat the egg whites until stiff, fold in the remaining sugar and cover the rice with the meringue topping. Cook in a slow oven, 300° F, 150° C, mark 2, for 15min. Serve hot.

Orange Upside-down Cake

2 oranges
2 tbsp (25ml, 2½ tbsp) golden syrup
3oz (75g, 6 tbsp) butter
3oz (75g, ⅓ cup) castor sugar
2 eggs
5oz (125g, 1¼ cups) self-raising flour

Preparation time: about 30min   Cooking time: 45min

Grate the rind and squeeze out the juice from an orange. Finely peel and slice second orange and remove the pips. Grease a 7in (17·75cm) cake tin and pour in the golden syrup. Arrange the sliced orange in the cake tin. Beat the butter and castor sugar together until light and creamy. Beat in the eggs and fold in the flour, adding the grated orange rind and juice and a little milk, if necessary, to make a dropping consistency. Pour the mixture into the cake tin and bake in a moderate oven, 350° F, 180° C, mark 4, for 45min. Turn out on to a serving plate so the orange slices are on the top. Serve hot or cold.

Orange Water Ice

8oz (250g, 1 cup) sugar
1pt (500ml, 2½ cups) water
½pt (250ml, 1¼ cups) fresh orange juice
2 tbsp (25ml, 2½ tbsp) fresh lemon juice
1 tbsp (10g, 1¼ tbsp) grated orange rind

Preparation time: about 25min   Cooking time: 6min
Chilling time: 3hr

Put the sugar and water in a saucepan and bring to the boil, then boil for 6min. Allow to cool. Strain the orange and lemon juice and pour into the sugar syrup, stirring in the grated orange rind. Put the mixture into the ice trays taken from the 'fridge, put the trays into the freezing compartment and allow the water ice to freeze for 30min.

Take the ice trays from the 'fridge and stir the water ice with a fork. Replace in the 'fridge and freeze for a further 30min. Remove and stir again. Replace the ice trays in the freezing compartment and re-freeze for 2hr. Turn out and serve with fan-shaped wafer biscuits.

Paskha (Russian Easter Pudding)

¾lb (375g, 1½ cups) cream cheese
2 eggs
2oz (50g, ¼ cup) castor sugar
2oz (50g, ½ cup) almond nibs
1oz (25g, 1 tbsp) raisins
1oz (25g, ⅓ cup) candied peel
1oz (25g, ¼ cup) glacé cherries
1oz (25g, ¼ cup) angelica
¼pt (125ml, scant ¾ cup) double cream
½ tsp (¾ tsp) vanilla essence
2oz (50g, 4 tbsp) butter

Preparation time: about 1hr   Chilling time: overnight
Wash thoroughly clean 5in high (12·75cm) flower pot and line with
a fine muslin cloth. Finely chop the candied peel, glacé cherries and
angelica. Separate the egg yolks from the egg whites. Whisk the
yolks and half the sugar until creamy and white. Stir in the vanilla
essence. Cream the butter and remaining sugar until creamy and white
and whisk into the egg yolks. Add the almond nibs, raisins, candied
peel, glacé cherries, angelica and whisk in the cream cheese. Beat the
cream until thick and whisk the egg whites until stiff. Fold the cream
and egg whites into the cream cheese mixture. Put the cream cheese
mixture into the prepared flower pot, wrap the muslin over the top
and put a heavy weight on the top. Put the flower pot into the 'fridge
or a cold place and leave overnight. Next day, turn out the paskha and
decorate with glacé cherries and angelica.

Poor Knights of Windsor

8 slices white bread
2 eggs
2oz (50g, ¼ cup) castor sugar
½pt (250ml, 1¼ cups) white wine
1 tsp (1¼ tsp) cinnamon
3oz (75g, 6 tbsp) butter

Preparation time: about 40min   Cooking time: 5min
Put the white wine and half the sugar into a shallow dish and soak the

slices of bread for 30min. Drain. Whisk the eggs lightly. Stir the cinnamon and remaining sugar together. Melt the butter. Dip the bread in the egg and fry in the melted butter on both sides until golden brown. Drain the bread on kitchen paper and sprinkle with the cinnamon and sugar. Serve hot.

Queen of Puddings

2 eggs
1 lemon
1pt (500ml, 2½ cups) milk
4oz (100g, 3 cups) white breadcrumbs
1oz (25g, 2 tbsp) butter
4oz (100g, ½ cup) castor sugar
3 tbsp (50ml, 4 tbsp) jam

Preparation time: about 1½hr   Cooking time: 55min

Separate the egg yolks from the whites. Grate the rind from the lemon and put into a bowl with the breadcrumbs and half the sugar. Heat the milk and pour into the bowl with the breadcrumbs. Leave to stand for 1hr. Whisk the egg yolks and stir them into the milk and breadcrumbs. Grease a 2pt pie dish, pour in the mixture and cook in a moderate oven, 325° F, 165° C, mark 3, for 45min. Heat the jam and spread it over the pudding. Whisk the egg whites until stiff and fold in the remaining sugar. Pile the meringue topping over the jam and cook for a further 10min in a slow oven, 300° F, 150° C, mark 2. Serve hot.

Sospiri (Italian Almond Biscuits)

4oz (100g, 1 cup) almond nibs
1 egg white
4oz (100g, ¾ cup) icing sugar
2 sheets rice paper

Preparation time: about 40min   Cooking time: 10min

Put the almond nibs on to a baking sheet and bake in a moderate oven, 350° F, 180° C, mark 4, for 5min. Whisk the egg white until very stiff, fold in the icing sugar and almond nibs and leave for 30min. Place the rice paper on a cake rack. Heat some oil, drop 1 tsp of the almond mixture into the hot oil and cook for about 1min. Remove the almond biscuits with a drainer spoon and put them on the rice paper. Leave the biscuits to go cold and serve with ice-cream.

Treacle Tart

8oz (250g, 2 cups) plain flour
4oz (100g, ½ cup) fat
4oz (100g, 3 cups) white breadcrumbs
12 tbsp (175ml, 1 cup) golden syrup

Preparation time: about 30min   Cooking time: 40min

Grease a 9in (23cm) pie plate. Make the shortcrust pastry (see page 11). Roll out the dough and line the pie plate, putting some dough aside to make a lattice top. Mix together the breadcrumbs and golden syrup, and pour into the prepared pastry case. Cut strips of pastry and lay them across the top of the breadcrumbs and golden syrup in a lattice pattern. Bake in a moderate oven, 350° F, 180° C, mark 4, for 40min. Serve hot or cold.

INDEX